IMAGES
of Aviation

ALBUQUERQUE INTERNATIONAL SUNPORT

The original Albuquerque Municipal Airport administration building of 1939 has been preserved and is now listed in the National Register of Historic Places. It is currently used for local offices of the Transportation Security Administration (TSA) but is open to the public during normal business hours. (Photograph by author.)

ON THE COVER: This Continental Air Lines Douglas DC-3 is departing from the original terminal of the Albuquerque Municipal Airport in the late 1940s. TWA (Transcontinental and Western Air) and Continental were the leaders of all commercial airlines at Albuquerque for over 50 years, providing the most service and building the airport into what it is today. (Albuquerque Museum.)

IMAGES
of Aviation

ALBUQUERQUE INTERNATIONAL SUNPORT

Fred De Guio

ARCADIA
PUBLISHING

Published by Arcadia Publishing
Charleston, South Carolina

Library of Congress Control Number: 2018964533

For all general information, please contact Arcadia Publishing:
Telephone 843-853-2070
Fax 843-853-0044
E-mail sales@arcadiapublishing.com
For customer service and orders:
Toll-Free 1-888-313-2665

Visit us on the Internet at www.arcadiapublishing.com

*To my late father, Alfred De Guio, for handing down
his knowledge of and historical interest in commercial
aviation at the Albuquerque Sunport.*

CONTENTS

ACKNOWLEDGMENTS

Many sources have helped with this pursuit, and I am truly grateful to all. I'll begin with Tom Norwood and Jon Proctor, commercial aviation historians and writers; Harry Davidson and David Straub, historians from the Cavalcade of Wings; the Albuquerque Museum, which supplied many historical photographs from the collection of Frank Speakman, the man who initiated the construction of the first Albuquerque Airport in 1928; Bjorn Larsson and David Zekria, for the use of many airline route maps included on their website, Timetableimages.com; Jon Jamieson for the use of photographs from his website, Departedwings.com; Peter Pierotti, attorney for the Albuquerque International Sunport; Joseph T. Page II, for help in writing; Michael Howell, for proofreading and editing; the staff at Picture Perfect, for photograph editing; and the many photographers who have captured images at the Albuquerque Sunport over the years and whose photographs are credited with their names.

All photographs without credit were taken by the author or are from the author's collection. Most images were taken at the Albuquerque International Sunport.

Again, thanks to all who have helped to document and remember the history of the Albuquerque International Sunport.

INTRODUCTION

The first airplane activity recorded at the city of Albuquerque occurred in October 1911, when aviator Charles F. Walsh landed a Model D pusher biplane on a track at the New Mexico Territorial Fair. New Mexico was still a territory at the time and was admitted as the 47th state the following year. After that, aircraft would land occasionally at suitable areas around Albuquerque, and it was not until the late 1920s that aviation had developed to a point where an airport was considered for the city.

Albuquerque's first airport opened in 1928, and within the first year, two commercial airlines, Western Air Express and Transcontinental Air Transport, had established regular service. The airport was rather close to the Sandia Mountains on the city's east side, causing a safety concern for Western Air Express, so that carrier chose to build its own airport on Albuquerque's west side. As the Great Depression settled in during 1930, the overlapping routes of the two carriers were merged, and the new entity was renamed TWA, providing a transcontinental route between Los Angeles and New York for passengers and mail. All operations were then moved to the west side airport, which became known as the TWA Airport.

Continental Airlines began service in the mid-1930s with a north-south route, also using the TWA Airport, and Albuquerque became a crossroads for air travel in the Southwest.

In 1939, the city opened its own municipal airport at a more ideal location, which is referenced as ABQ and continues to be used today. Both TWA and Continental Airlines then moved to the new Albuquerque Municipal Airport. During World War II, the airport was used extensively by the military, at which time the Albuquerque Army Airfield was established at the same site. The airfield went on to become Kirtland Air Force Base and is one of only a few airfields in the United States today that is shared between military and civilian activities.

After the war, the airport quickly began to see more airlines, new routes, and much larger aircraft. Four-engine jets began parking at the small terminal building by 1961, and a much larger terminal was opened in 1965. At that time, there were four airlines serving the city, and all four were operating jets within two years after the new terminal, nicknamed the "Sunport," became operational.

Many other airlines applied to the Civil Aeronautics Board (an agency created in 1938 to regulate the route structures of the airlines) to serve Albuquerque through the 1970s, but it was not until airline deregulation was passed in late 1978 that the city saw any new activity. New airlines then flooded the airport through the 1980s, building ticket counters anywhere there was space and having airplanes double up at the gates. Most gates did not have jet bridges until a massive expansion and modernization of the terminal was done in the late 1980s.

Among the new carriers to begin service was Southwest Airlines in 1980, with flights to Dallas Love Field. Southwest quickly added more flights and destinations and, within two years, had taken over the top spot as the busiest carrier at ABQ. Southwest went on to create a small hub at the airport with as many as 66 departing flights per day. The airline has since downsized and now has a much smaller operation; however, it is still by far the busiest carrier serving Albuquerque.

The total number of daily departing flights of all carriers at ABQ has been as high as 164, and nonstop service has been seen to at least 76 cities within the United States and Mexico. Overall passenger traffic at the airport peaked in 2007 with 6.7 million passengers, and although traffic then slipped after a recession took hold of the country, it has been slowly rebounding in recent years.

This book will take a look at each of the airports used commercially in Albuquerque since 1928 and examine all the commercial air carriers that have served these airports, with emphasis on their route systems and aircraft used. The importance of ABQ as a hub to all of the smaller rural communities throughout New Mexico will be covered, as will the charter airlines, freighters, general aviation, and non-scheduled activities that have occurred at the Sunport. Some of the special events and tragic events will also be noted.

One

ALBUQUERQUE AIRPORT
1928–1930

After Col. Charles Lindbergh made his solo nonstop crossing of the Atlantic Ocean in 1927, Albuquerque resident Frank G. Speakman became so deeply inspired by aviation that he took it upon himself to build an airport for his home city. He and partner William Langford Franklin leased 140 acres of land about six miles southeast of downtown Albuquerque. Both men were working night shifts at the Santa Fe Railway and began construction in early 1928 during their daylight downtime. They acquired a used tractor and grader, but construction moved very slowly as the equipment was inadequate for the job. Speakman and Franklin then approached Albuquerque mayor Clyde Tingley for assistance. The mayor was in favor of the project but had no funds in the treasury for such a purpose, so he offered the men the use of city equipment at night. Speakman quit his job and devoted himself full time to constructing the airfield. On May 15, 1928, the first aircraft landed at the new airport, soon followed by others including a large Ford tri-motor operated by Scenic Airways. Although this was a private venture, the airfield was named the Albuquerque Airport.

By July 1928, a man by the name of James G. Oxnard appeared on the scene and bought out the interest that Langford Franklin had in the new airfield. Oxnard then quickly invested in the airport to build it into a first-class field by constructing an administration building and the first hangar. Frank Speakman would be the airport manager, and he and his wife would live in the administration building.

In early 1929, the field was expanded to 480 acres, and the runways were extended. Lighting was installed for night operations, and a clubhouse was built followed by a second and much larger hangar. In mid-1929, two airlines—Western Air Express and Transcontinental Air Transport—began service with competing routes, but would use the airport for only a short time before moving to another new airfield on Albuquerque's west mesa. The Albuquerque Airport then unofficially became known as Oxnard Field servicing general aviation.

The first Albuquerque Airport opened in mid-1928, although several aircraft had already been landing on the incomplete runways. About one year after opening, a public display was featured, seen here, showing many improvements including the installation of ramp and runway lighting. (Albuquerque Museum.)

The first two structures at the airport were a traditional Southwest-style adobe administration building and one small hangar. Instead of pavement, the airport's tarmac and runways were coated with oil. (Albuquerque Museum.)

Frank Speakman (left), founder of the Albuquerque Airport, stands alongside Mayor Clyde Tingley (center) and airport chief pilot "Bill" Cutter in front of the airport administration building. Cutter would later begin a charter business called Cutter Flying Service. (Albuquerque Museum.)

Western Air Express (WAE) made a trial run landing at the new Albuquerque Airport with this Fokker F-10 tri-motor in late 1928. The carrier later announced its intentions to provide commercial passenger service to the city. Special events such as this attracted hundreds of onlookers, many of whom would gather around the aircraft even with engines running. (Albuquerque Museum.)

WAE began the first commercial flight to Albuquerque from Los Angeles on May 15, 1929, using the Fokker F-10 tri-motor. Two weeks later, the route was extended eastward to Kansas City. (Albuquerque Museum.)

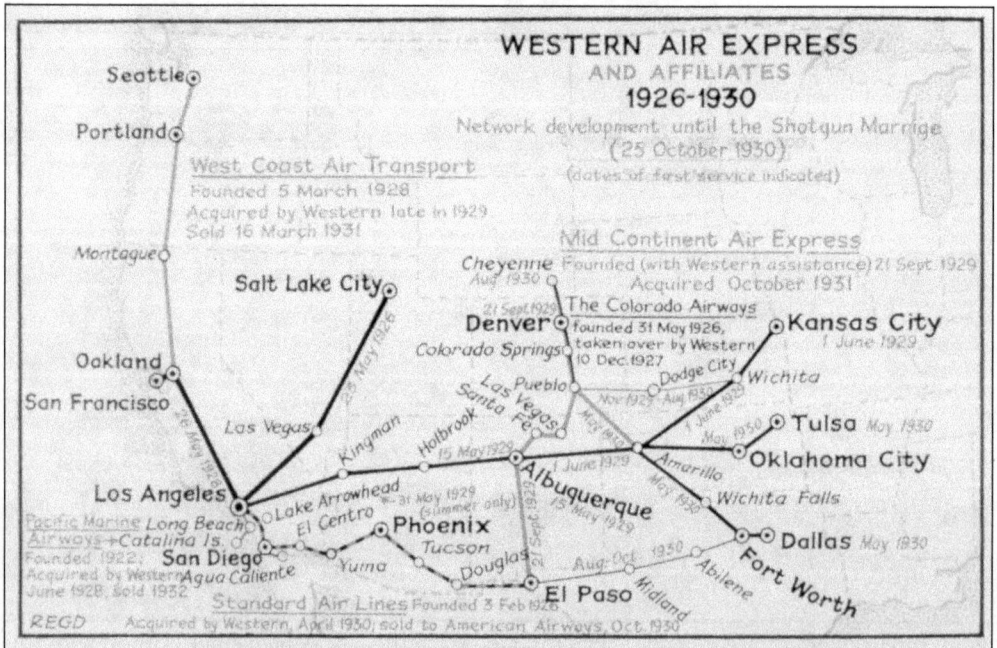

This WAE route map from 1930 shows the many routes that WAE operated, including the Los Angeles–Kansas City route, with stops in Kingman and Holbrook, then Albuquerque, Amarillo, and Wichita.

Transcontinental Air Transport (TAT) was the second airline to serve Albuquerque. The carrier, in cooperation with two railroad companies, began a coast to coast service with the first scheduled flights landing at Albuquerque on July 9, 1929. TAT operated a fleet of 12-passenger Ford F-5AT tri-motor aircraft, one of which was christened the *City of Albuquerque*. The journey from Los Angeles to New York took roughly 48 hours, about half the time it took to make the entire trip by train. (Albuquerque Museum.)

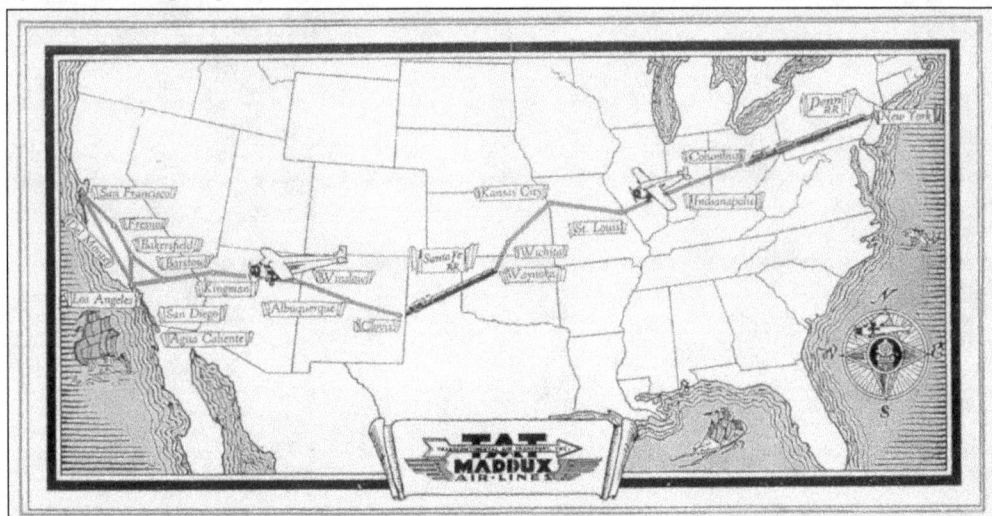

TAT's initial route map shows all ports of call as well as the two segments operated at night by trains. Due to the lack of navigational aids at the time, aircraft could not fly safely at night. Clovis, New Mexico, and Waynoka, Oklahoma, were chosen as stops due to their proximity to the railroad and the schedule of the trains providing continuous service throughout the night. Within a few months, TAT had merged with Maddux Airlines of California, giving the carrier new routes in the West, including an extension from Los Angeles to San Francisco, as indicated on this map from late 1929.

13

TAT built its own terminal, shown here, which included a covered walkway that was extendable to the aircraft. The carrier also chose Albuquerque to be its western division headquarters. (Albuquerque Museum.)

This is a view of the interior of the TAT terminal, with its Southwestern décor including native Indian artifacts. TAT went to great expense to provide the most comfortable service and accommodations for its passengers. (Albuquerque Museum.)

Charles Lindbergh (left) and TAT field manager Arthur Horton walk through the canopy leading from the TAT terminal to the aircraft. Lindbergh had become the technical advisor for TAT and determined the route the airline would fly. (Albuquerque Museum.)

Seen here is the University of New Mexico football team of 1929 departing for the Rose Bowl game in Pasadena, California. A second TAT Ford tri-motor was needed to transport the entire team. (Albuquerque Museum.)

A clubhouse called the Airport Inn was constructed between the administration building and the TAT terminal. It provided dining, a lounge, a soda fountain, and entertainment features for passengers, pilots, and visitors. (Albuquerque Museum.)

This aerial view of the Albuquerque Airport faces east. The original hangar is at the bottom of the row of buildings, followed by the second and much larger hangar. The administration building is partially obscured by the larger hangar, then the Airport Inn and a small unidentified building. Farther up is the TAT terminal and another small unidentified building. The original hangar had the name "Albuquerque Airport" written on the roof, which was a common practice for airports at a time when pilots had very few navigational aids. (Albuquerque Museum.)

Albuquerque was on the Los Angeles–Amarillo airway (roughly following US Highway 66, or today's Interstate 40), and for navigation, airway beacons and cement directional arrows were constructed on the ground at 10-mile intervals. Emergency landing sites were built about every 50 miles. The first landing strip west of Albuquerque, shown here, was at Acomita, New Mexico. Some of the buildings, equipment, and the beacon have since been relocated to nearby Grants, New Mexico, and are now displayed at the Airway Heritage Museum sponsored by the Cibola County Historical Society at the Grants airport. (Paul and Terry Freeman.)

Despite exhaustive efforts by TAT to retrieve accurate weather data for safe flying, a TAT tri-motor crashed in severe storms on Mt. Taylor, 60 miles west of Albuquerque and a few miles north of the Acomita site mentioned above. The accident happened on September 3, 1929, less than two months after TAT began service. There were no survivors.

A group of aviators and local dignitaries are seen here in front of a TAT tri-motor at Albuquerque on July 14, 1929. Standing third from the left is Amelia Earhart, the first female aviator to fly solo across the Atlantic Ocean. Second from the right is Albuquerque mayor Clyde Tingley. (Albuquerque Museum.)

Shown here is an aerial view of the Albuquerque Airport in 1948. The two air carriers left the airport by 1930, and the field was then primarily used for general aviation until it was acquired by the Army upon the outbreak of World War II. After the war ended in 1945, hundreds of excess aircraft were flown here, as seen in this photograph, and ultimately dismantled. (Albuquerque Museum.)

Two

WAE, TWA Airport

1929–1939

The second airfield to serve Albuquerque was constructed by Western Air Express (WAE), opening in the fall of 1929 and initially called the WAE Airport. The new facility had treated dirt runways, which was typical for airfields at the time. About the same time of the move to the new airport, WAE helped create an offshoot airline called Mid-Continent Air Express (MCAE), which began a north-south route from Denver to El Paso that included stops at Albuquerque, Santa Fe, and Las Vegas, New Mexico. This made Albuquerque a crossroads for air travel in the Southwest. As it turned out, the city was served by two commercial airports until mid-1930, when the Los Angeles–Kansas City route of WAE (the route that served Albuquerque) was merged with its competing carrier, Transcontinental Air Transport (TAT). TAT's operation was then moved from the Albuquerque Airport to the WAE Airport, and the newly merged carrier became known as Transcontinental and Western Air, or TWA. The WAE Airport then took on the name TWA Airport. The merger was necessary in order to obtain a US mail contract that both carriers needed to survive during a time when the Great Depression was taking a tight grip on the country. On October 25, 1930, the mail contract took effect and the use of the two overnight trains ended, as the transcontinental route was now able to be served entirely by air. The stops in Clovis and Waynoka also ended, and passengers spent one night in Kansas City before flying on to New York the next day. The TWA Airport terminal was expanded with a lounge area and an extendable canopy to the aircraft, identical to what was used at the TAT terminal at the Albuquerque Airport.

Varney Speed Lines began service in 1934 by obtaining a mail contract for the north-south route and taking over the service previously flown by WAE. The carrier changed its name to Continental Air Lines in mid-1937. The two airlines, TWA and Continental, continued to serve the TWA Airport until July 1939, when the area received exceptional monsoon rains that flooded the dirt runways. A new Albuquerque Municipal Airport was nearing completion at the time, so aircraft were diverted to the paved runways of this new facility. A decision was quickly made to move all operations to the new airport while work was still in progress.

The Western Air Express (WAE) Airport opened in 1929, also with a small adobe administration building and a large hangar. The larger aircraft in the foreground is a WAE Fokker F-10, and the smaller aircraft is a Fokker F-8 Super Universal operated by Mid-Continent Air Express. (Albuquerque Museum.)

This aerial view shows the WAE Airport with its three dirt runways. The runways all intersected at the center, creating a star-like pattern. The dark bluffs in the background are now Petroglyph National Monument. (Albuquerque Museum.)

20

Mid-Continent Air Express (MCAE) began a north-south route in September 1929, linking Albuquerque with Denver and El Paso. Pictured here is an MCAE single-engine Fokker F-8 Super Universal at the Denver Municipal Airport. The carrier was absorbed by WAE in 1931, which continued serving the route for three more years. This north-south route is also indicated on the map on page 12. (Delta Flight Museum in Atlanta, Georgia.)

Shown here is a Ford tri-motor in front of the small adobe terminal, now in the markings of TWA (Transcontinental and Western Air) after TAT and the Los Angeles–Kansas City division of WAE were merged. (Albuquerque Museum.)

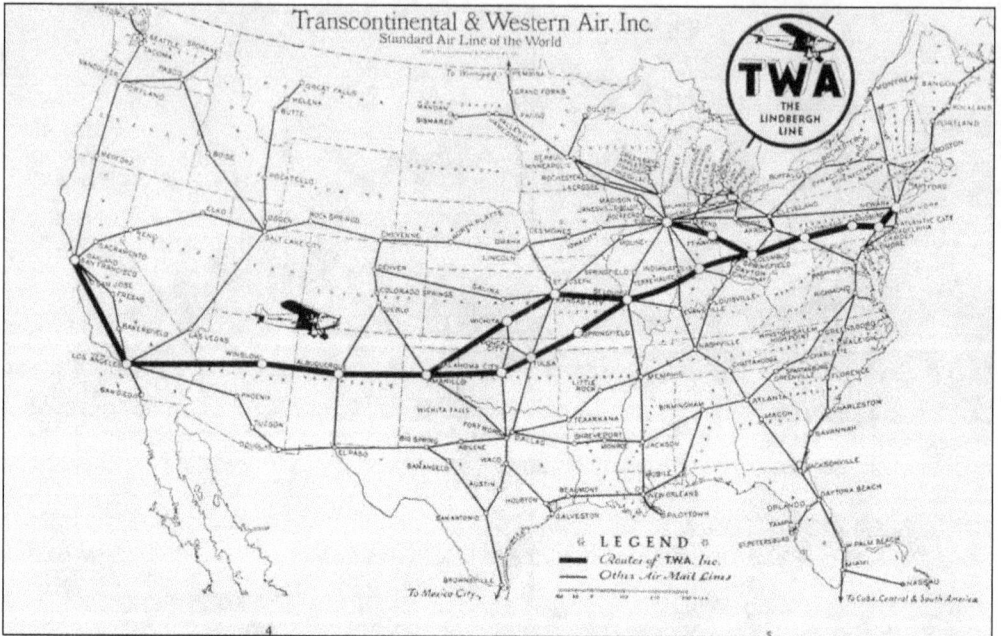

This TWA route map from 1932 shows the new routing of the carrier's transcontinental line, now stopping in Amarillo rather than Clovis and Waynoka. New routes to San Francisco, Chicago, and through Oklahoma had been added by this time, while the stop at Kingman, Arizona, was discontinued. (Bjorn Larsson.)

TWA introduced the 14-passenger Douglas DC-2, seen here, in 1934, which was a leap forward in speed and comfort over the tri-motor aircraft previously operated. TWA billed itself as "the Lindbergh Line" in honor of famous aviator Charles Lindbergh, who was instrumental in creating the airline in 1929.

The TWA Airport is pictured in the mid-1930s with the new DC-2 parked on the tarmac. The terminal/administration building had been expanded by this time with the addition of a lounge on the east side. (Albuquerque Museum.)

This is the interior lounge of the TWA Airport terminal containing the native furnishings and artifacts from the vacated TAT terminal at the Albuquerque Airport. (Albuquerque Museum.)

In 1934, Varney Speed Lines took over the north-south route formerly operated by Western Air Express. Varney only operated the route as far north as Pueblo, Colorado, and passengers then connected with Wyoming Air Service to continue to Denver. From Denver, the Wyoming Air Service flights continued north through Cheyenne, Casper, and Sheridan, Wyoming, ending in Billings, Montana. Seen here are the route maps of Varney Speed Lines (left) and Wyoming Air Service (right). (Bjorn Larsson.)

Varney's initial aircraft was the Lockheed 5 Vega, which could carry four passengers but mainly carried US mail. The north-south route connected with the east-west transcontinental routes of TWA at Albuquerque, with American Airlines at El Paso, with United Air Lines at Cheyenne, and with Northwest Airlines at Billings. This photograph of a Lockheed Vega was taken in 1964 as the carrier was commemorating its 30th anniversary. (Albuquerque Museum.)

Varney Speed Lines was changed to Continental Air Lines on July 1, 1937. Shown here is the cover of the first Continental timetable, which lists the cities served. By this time, Continental received authority to fly the north-south route back up to Denver, and United Air Lines had added Denver onto its transcontinental route, allowing passengers to connect with United there rather than Cheyenne. The stop at Las Vegas, New Mexico, was suspended but restarted a couple years later. (Bjorn Larsson.)

Fly The Old Santa Fé Trail CONTINENTAL AIR LINES

DENVER · EL PASO
ALBUQUERQUE
SANTA FE · PUEBLO
COLORADO SPRINGS

Effective July 1, 1937

Varney had upgraded its fleet with 10-seat Lockheed Electras shortly before becoming Continental Air Lines. This was the same aircraft type that famous aviator Amelia Earhart flew in her attempt to travel around the world in 1937. (Albuquerque Museum.)

This photograph of the TWA Airport shows both the terminal and the TWA hangar. The canopy that was extended to the TWA aircraft can also be seen. The aircraft on the far left with a fuel truck parked in front of it appears to be a Continental Lockheed Electra. (Albuquerque Museum.)

After the air carriers moved out in mid-1939, the TWA Airport then became known as the West Mesa Airport. Cutter Flying Service had moved to this airport in the mid-1930s, and in 1939, Bill Cutter teamed up with fellow pilot Clark Carr, renaming Cutter's business to Cutter-Carr Flying Service. The service handled all airport operations until Carr separated from the partnership in 1947. Cutter later moved to the new municipal airport but maintained limited services at the West Mesa Airport until the field was closed in 1967. (Albuquerque Museum.)

Three

ALBUQUERQUE MUNICIPAL AIRPORT
1939–1965

In 1935, the city of Albuquerque, with support from TWA, decided that a new municipal airport was needed and money from a Works Progress Administration (WPA) grant was obtained for its construction. A new parcel of land on the city's east side was acquired, which was three miles west and farther from the mountains of the original Albuquerque Airport. The new $700,000 facility began operating on July 29, 1939, complete with paved runways, an adobe-style terminal, and a large hangar designed to accommodate upcoming four-engine aircraft. TWA and Continental then moved their operations and 12 daily flights to the new airfield, named the Albuquerque Municipal Airport. The terminal was operated by TWA and referred to as the TWA administration building. This new location, coded as ABQ, is still in use today.

As World War II was erupting in Europe, the Albuquerque Army Air Base (later Kirtland Air Force Base) was constructed east of the terminal and completed only months before the United States entered the war in late 1941. After the war, two new airlines began serving the airport; Monarch Air Lines in 1947 with a route to Salt Lake City, and Pioneer Air Lines in 1948 with a route to Dallas. The four airlines were operating 38 flights per day, all with Douglas DC-3 aircraft, until late 1948, when TWA introduced the tri-tailed Lockheed Constellation and Continental began flying the larger Convair 240. The first air taxi, Carco, also began service with flights to Los Alamos, New Mexico. Several additions were made to the terminal, providing more operational space. Monarch became Frontier Airlines in 1950 and Pioneer merged into Continental in 1955. By 1959, Continental introduced the four-engine Vickers Viscount, and Frontier began flying the Convair 340. Albuquerque's population had more than doubled during the 1950s, growing from 96,000 to 201,000. TWA began the first jet service in 1961, with both the Boeing 707 and the Convair 880, followed closely by Continental with the Boeing 720. In late 1963, Trans-Texas Airways came to ABQ to take over the service to many of the smaller cities in New Mexico that Continental had been serving. TWA, Continental, Frontier, and Trans-Texas (later Texas International) were the four legacy airlines that served Albuquerque through the 1970s. The airport was renamed the Albuquerque Sunport in 1963.

The new terminal building is nearing completion in 1939. (Albuquerque Museum.)

The runways are under construction in February 1939. There would be four runways, 08-26, 17-35, 03-21, and 11-29, representing the compass heading for the direction of each runway by adding a "0" after each number. This photograph faces east and shows the east-west runway (08-26) and the north-south runway (17-35) crossing at center, with the terminal and hangar at lower left. (Albuquerque Museum.)

The new terminal and the TWA hangar were completed in mid-1939. Both structures are still in use today; however, the hangar was relocated to the south side of the main east-west runway in 1970. It is hard to fathom how a structure this size could withstand such a move and remain structurally stable for over 80 years now. (Albuquerque Museum.)

This local news article reported the opening of the new municipal airport. It was scheduled to open on August 15, 1939, but began receiving flights a few weeks early due to flooding from torrential rain at the old TWA Airport on the west mesa.

September, 1939   ALBUQUERQUE PROGRESS   Page 7

NEW $700,000 AIRPORT NOW IN USE

Albuquerque's new municipal airport is now being occupied by TWA and Continental Airlines, and the U. S. Army air detachment which serves army and navy planes.

The Weather Bureau officials have moved all weather observation equipment to the new port where official weather observations are now being made.

This is an iconic photograph of a TWA DC-3 with people freely walking the ramp and admiring the aircraft. Local Native Americans would greet passengers and sell or trade their pottery and crafts on the tarmac. (Albuquerque Museum.)

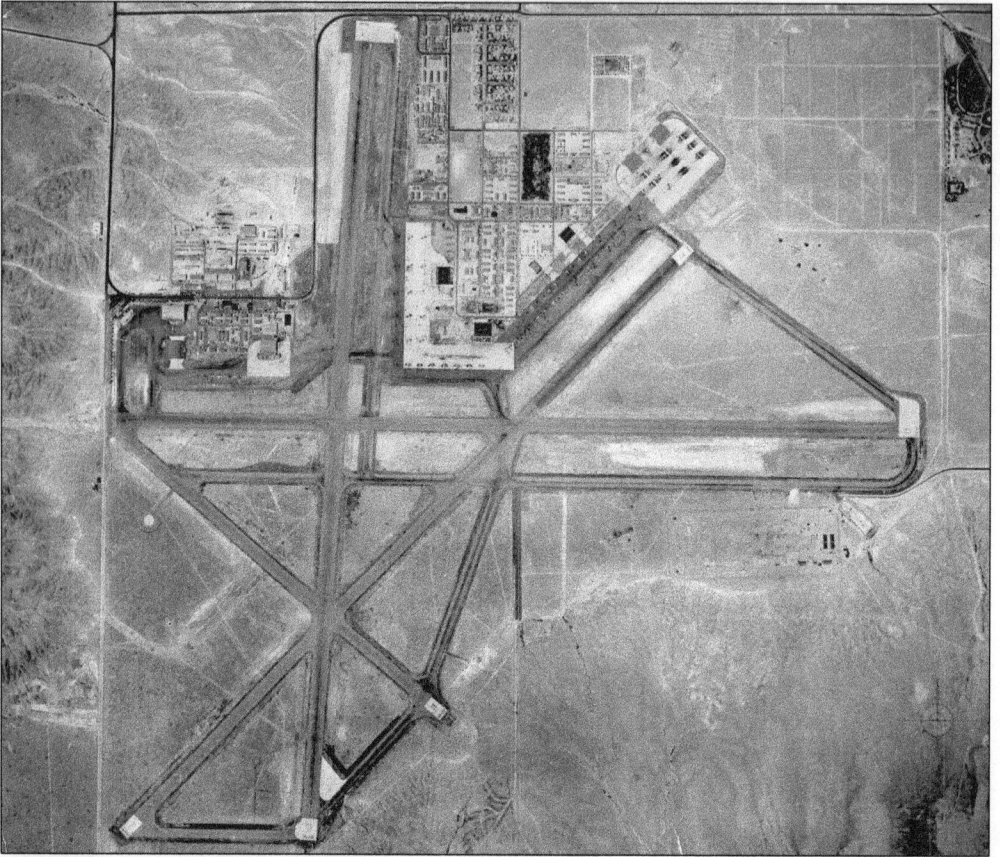

Seen here is an aerial view of the new airport in 1945, with its four paved runways, looking north. The Albuquerque Army Airfield (later Kirtland Field and then Kirtland Air Force Base) was built shortly after the terminal opened and occupies all of the new development east of the north-south runway. The east-west runway, 08-26, was later lengthened to the east for a total distance of 13,793 feet, making it one of the longest in the world. (Albuquerque Museum.)

Albuquerque mayor Clyde Tingley is seen here disembarking from a TWA DC-3. Introduced in 1937, the 21-seat DC-3s replaced the DC-2s and became the workhorse for TWA and most other airlines through the 1940s and into the 1950s. Some aircraft were equipped with sleeping berths and could be flown all night for continuous coast-to-coast flights. (Albuquerque Museum.)

TWA introduced the four-engine Boeing 307 Stratoliner in 1940, able to carry 33 passengers. The aircraft flew nonstop from Los Angeles to Albuquerque and then on to Kansas City, Chicago, and New York, making a coast-to-coast journey in 13 hours and 40 minutes with only three stops. Unfortunately, the Stratoliners, as well as many other civilian aircraft, were soon assigned to serve the military during the war years of 1941 through 1945. After the war, the aircraft returned to service with TWA for a few more years in the late 1940s. TWA instructors trained more than 1,100 pilots for the Army as World War II began. (Albuquerque Museum.)

In 1946, TWA acquired a second type of four-engine aircraft, the Douglas DC-4. These aircraft were soon converted to freighters, designated C-54s, and served ABQ with all cargo flights in the early 1950s. By this time, TWA had changed its name to Trans World Airlines, keeping the same letters. (Albuquerque Museum.)

Under the control of famous aviator Howard Hughes, TWA ultimately decided upon the four-engine, 57-passenger Lockheed Constellation, nicknamed the "Connie," to be the mainstay for its fleet. The first in a series of Connies to be operated by TWA was this model L-049, which began serving ABQ in 1948. Connies were used on most flights through ABQ during the 1950s. (Albuquerque Museum.)

The unique triple-tail design of the Connie is seen here as a TWA flight is deplaning passengers at ABQ in 1949. With traffic increasing dramatically after World War II, a second level was added to the terminal. (Albuquerque Museum.)

In the early 1950s, TWA replaced its fleet of DC-3s with Martin 404 airliners. The Martin 404, pictured here, was flown through Albuquerque twice per day, once eastbound and once westbound. Santa Fe was also served on these flights through the 1950s. The Martin fleet was retired by 1961.

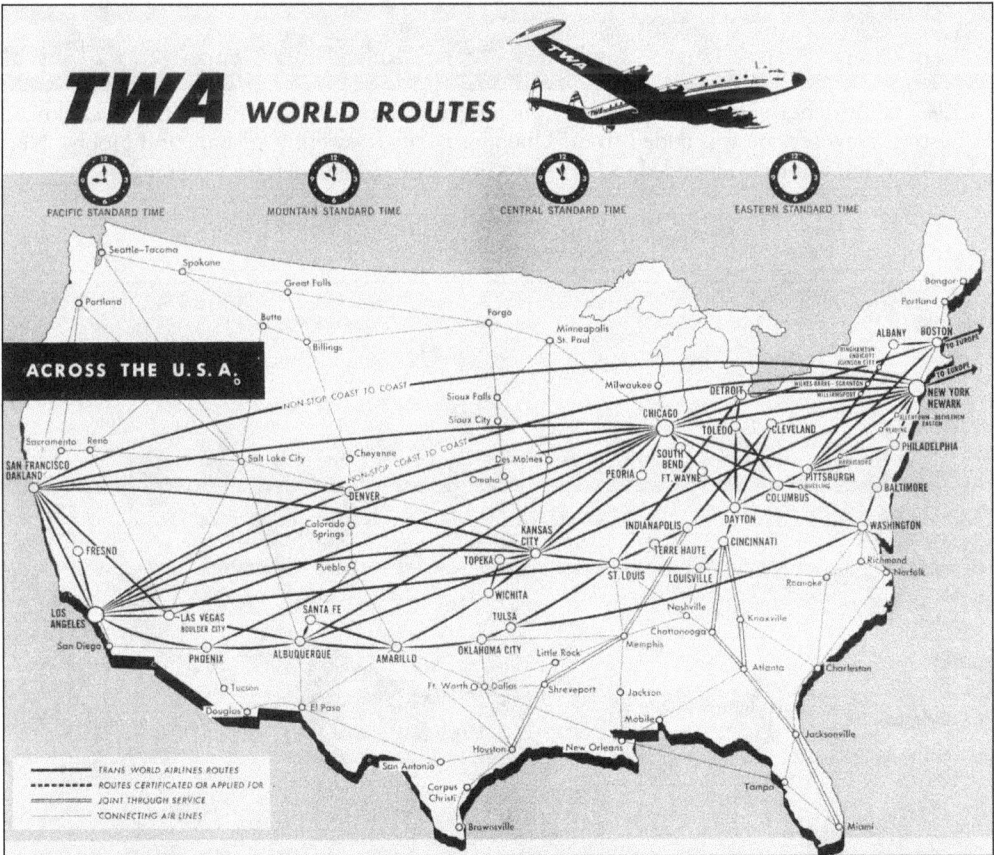

By 1956, TWA began flying nonstop to Chicago and was flying to six other cities from ABQ. New service to Phoenix and Las Vegas/Boulder City, Nevada, had begun, while the stop in Winslow, Arizona, had ended. Nonstop service to Los Angeles was also flown but not shown on this route map, and service to Tucson began shortly afterward. As airlines worked extensively with each other back then, their maps commonly showed the routes of many other carriers throughout the United States. (Bjorn Larsson.)

In 1940, Continental Air Lines upgraded from a fleet of Lockheed Electras to 18-seat Lockheed Lodestars. New service was added from Albuquerque to Roswell, Carlsbad, and Hobbs, New Mexico, which was later extended to San Antonio, Texas. (Albuquerque Museum.)

Continental then replaced its Lodestars with DC-3s by the mid-1940s. The DC-3s would continue to fly for the airline, serving smaller cities through 1963. (Albuquerque Museum.)

In 1949, Continental introduced the 40-seat Convair 240 (pictured) on several flights through ABQ and soon began nonstop flights to Denver with this aircraft. During the 1950s, the 240s were replaced with similar looking but slightly larger Convair 340s and 440s. (Albuquerque Museum.)

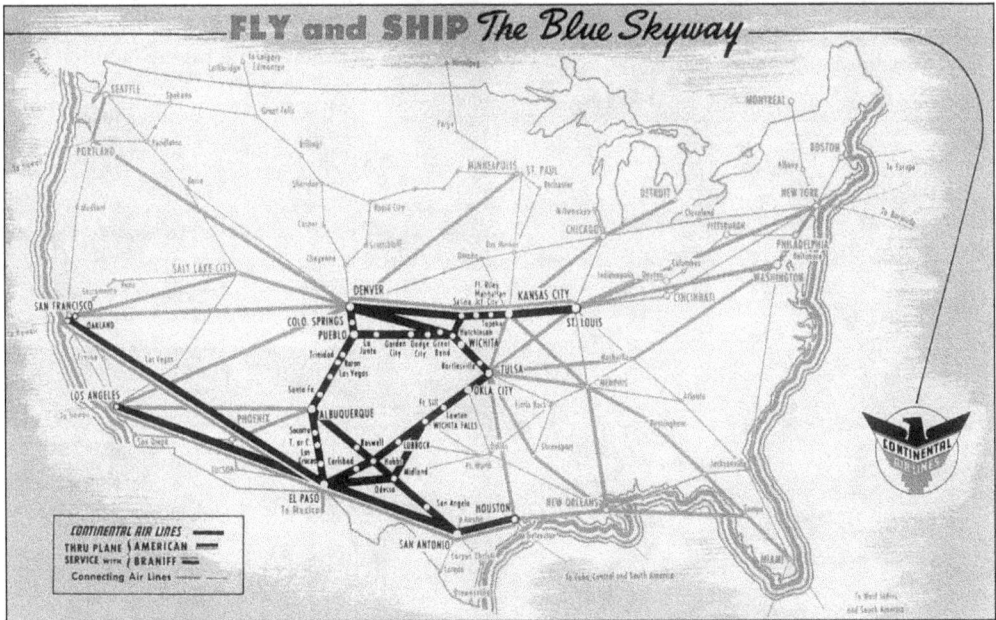

This route map from a Continental Air Lines timetable in 1952 shows the carrier's new routes as well as the many very small cities that were served at the time, such as Raton, Socorro, and Truth or Consequences (T or C), New Mexico. T or C had just changed its name from Hot Springs due to a publicity stunt by a popular radio quiz show at the time. All three cities, as well as Las Vegas and Las Cruces, New Mexico, were discontinued by 1955. (Bjorn Larsson.)

Pioneer Air Lines, designated as a local service airline, began a passenger and mail route from Albuquerque to Dallas in 1948. The route initially made seven stops, as seen on this map; however, the stops at Las Vegas and Tucumcari, New Mexico, were discontinued in the early 1950s. (Bjorn Larsson.)

Pioneer started flying with the DC-3, pictured here, and upgraded to 36-seat Martin 202 aircraft in 1952. The 202s were too expensive to operate, and Pioneer reverted back to DC-3s the following year, which were then reconfigured to hold 24 passengers. Pioneer merged into Continental Air Lines in 1955, giving Continental the authority to operate the highly lucrative route between Albuquerque and Dallas. (Albuquerque Museum.)

Monarch Air Lines was awarded a route from Albuquerque to Salt Lake City, which began in 1947. This route also initially made seven stops, as seen on this map. Upon reaching Durango, Colorado, passengers from Albuquerque could change planes to another flight to Denver or to any of the other many cities on that route. (Bjorn Larsson.)

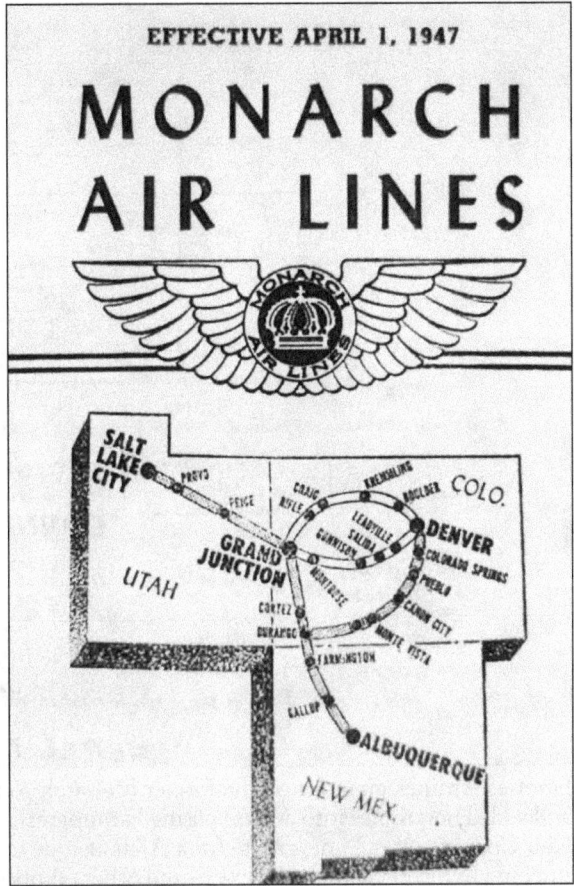

EFFECTIVE APRIL 1, 1947

MONARCH
AIR LINES

Monarch was also a local service airline primarily serving smaller cities using the Douglas DC-3, shown here. In 1950, Monarch merged with two other carriers to become Frontier Airlines. (Albuquerque Museum.)

Frontier Airlines maintained the former Monarch route from Albuquerque to Salt Lake City and added new routes into Arizona using Farmington, New Mexico, as a connecting hub for the Four Corners states. A new route from Albuquerque to Tucson and Phoenix was added in 1956, stopping in Silver City, New Mexico, and other points in Arizona, as seen on this Frontier route map from 1958. Frontier was also designated as a local service airline. (Bjorn Larsson.)

Frontier continued using DC-3s (seen here) and added a fleet of 44-passenger Convair 340s beginning in 1959. In 1963, a new direct route to Denver was added, stopping in Santa Fe and points in Colorado, as well as new flights to El Paso, stopping in Alamogordo, New Mexico. Both new routes were handed down from Continental Airlines. (Albuquerque Museum.)

Carco was the first air taxi or commuter airline in the United States, established in 1947 by Clark Carr, who previously partnered with Bill Cutter operating Cutter-Carr Flying Service. The carrier operated shuttle flights between Albuquerque and Los Alamos using Beech Bonanzas and other small aircraft shown here. This service was created to transport employees of the Atomic Energy Commission on official business. Los Alamos was a secret city at the time, established to develop atomic weapons. (Albuquerque Museum.)

At least three other commuter airlines are known to have served Albuquerque between 1958 and 1965. Bald Eagle, Bison, and Solar Airlines all connected Albuquerque with cities in southeast New Mexico and west Texas. Bald Eagle operated Beech 18 aircraft, while Bison flew Aero Commanders. Pictured here is a Solar Airlines Piper Seneca.

This view of the airport terminal lobby in February 1949 shows the TWA ticket counter on the left and the smaller Monarch Air Lines ticket counter on the right. At this time, Continental and Pioneer Air Lines, as well as Carco Air Taxi, were also serving the airport. TWA and Continental also had ticket offices at the Hilton (now the Hotel Andaluz) in downtown Albuquerque. The buffalo mural is still displayed in the terminal today. (Albuquerque Museum.)

Passengers are seen here exiting the terminal to board their flight in 1949. There was no security checkpoint at the time, and would not be for many years. (Albuquerque Museum.)

Passengers board a TWA DC-3 on a summer day in the late 1940s. The front of a Continental DC-3 can also be seen on the right. TWA and Continental flights carried both a flight number and a name, such as "Arrow King," "Chicagoan," "Mojave," and "Navajo." (Albuquerque Museum.)

There were times when TWA had multiple aircraft on the ground simultaneously. This early 1950s photograph shows two Connies and a DC-3 taxiing out in the center. (Albuquerque Museum.)

This photograph, also from the early 1950s, shows aircraft from three of the four carriers serving Albuquerque. From left to right are a Continental Convair 240, a TWA Constellation, and a Frontier DC-3. (Albuquerque Museum.)

The fourth carrier serving ABQ in the early 1950s was Pioneer Air Lines, whose larger Martin 202 aircraft is seen here. The triple tail of a TWA Connie can be seen at right. (Albuquerque Museum.)

Cutter-Carr Flying Service set up a new operation at the municipal airport in 1947, using this large hangar and a subsequent smaller hangar to the right. Cutter also ran an air-taxi operation through the 1960s. (Albuquerque Museum.)

A Ford tri-motor with the markings of TAT, one of the two carriers that became TWA, made a visit to Albuquerque in 1949 commemorating 20 years of TWA service. (Albuquerque Museum.)

Seen here is a traditional local Indian dance performed on the tarmac in 1950. There was little problem with holding large events on the tarmac at that time, as people were trusted to not interfere with aircraft operations. (Albuquerque Museum.)

The duke and duchess of Spain arrived in Albuquerque aboard a TWA Super Constellation in 1956 for a visit to the Duke City. Albuquerque was founded in 1706 and named for the Duke of Alburquerque, Spain. The first "r" was later dropped. (Albuquerque Museum.)

On the morning of February 19, 1955, TWA flight 260, a Martin 404 aircraft on a short flight to Santa Fe, crashed into the Sandia Mountains to the northeast of Albuquerque. Sandia Peak, reaching an elevation of 10,678 feet, lies directly in the flight path, and all 13 passengers and three crew members onboard were killed. Although it was cloudy over the mountains that morning, at first it was determined that the captain had intentionally steered the aircraft into the mountain. A fellow TWA pilot refused to believe the accusation and later proved that the fluxgate compass used on the Martin 404 had been giving erroneous readings on other TWA flights. Five years later, the captain of flight 260 was cleared of wrongdoing. Pictured above is Benjamin De Guio, who accompanied the author on a hike to the crash site, where some of the wreckage remains today high on the rocky western slope of the Sandia Mountains. The image below shows a memorial to flight 260 listing the names of the passengers and crew that is displayed in the former TWA Ambassadors Club (now the Sandia Vista room) at the Sunport.

This postcard of the Albuquerque Sunport in the early 1960s shows the terminal dwarfed by two large four-engine aircraft. TWA Constellations had regularly been flown through the airport since 1948, and Continental began service with its Vickers Viscount in 1959, followed soon by a Douglas DC-7. Large four-engine jets would soon follow.

The first commercial jets to service ABQ were the Boeing 707 and the Convair 880, both operated by TWA and both beginning on April 30, 1961. The Convair 880, pictured here on its inaugural visit, stopped at Albuquerque twice per day on a route from Chicago to Phoenix. The Boeing 707 flew a nonstop flight to Los Angeles.

For a short time in the summer of 1962, Continental operated a Boeing 720 (a slightly shorter version of the 707) for one daily flight each way on a Denver-Albuquerque-Midland/Odessa-Dallas routing.

In 1964, TWA introduced yet a third jetliner, the Boeing 727-100, and quickly replaced all remaining flights still flown with Connies, the carrier's last propeller-driven aircraft. By the end of 1964, TWA was operating all jets at the Albuquerque Sunport. Note the built-in stairwell underneath the tail of the 727. (Albuquerque Museum.)

In late 1963, Trans-Texas Airways, a local service airline, began service to Albuquerque by taking over Continental's routes to Santa Fe, Clovis, Roswell, Carlsbad, and Hobbs, New Mexico. Trans-Texas began using DC-3s (pictured) but soon upgraded some flights with larger Convair 240s. (Albuquerque Museum.)

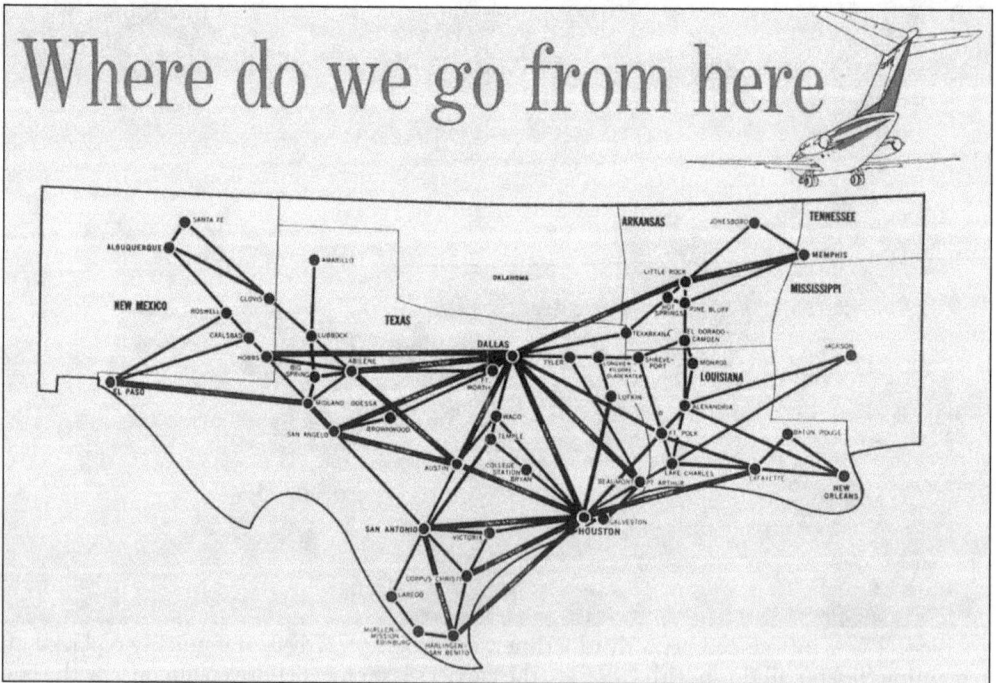

A Trans-Texas Airways route map from 1966 is seen here. Most flights originated in Albuquerque and ultimately continued to Dallas, with many stops in between.

Four

A New Terminal
for the Jet Age
1965–1979

On November 12, 1965, ABQ opened a new, $2.5 million, 176,000-square-foot terminal just east of the old terminal. The new facility had eight gates each able to handle a large jet. Four of the gates were at the main building, and the other four were in a satellite building to the south and connected to the main building by a tunnel underneath the aircraft apron. The facility was split level; after checking in, passengers had to go up one level to be on the ground level of the aircraft. A great hall lobby is in the center of the building on the upper level, which offered gift shops, barber and beauty shops, a coffee shop, an insurance booth, and a TV room. A fine restaurant was located on a third level overlooking the great hall. The terminal also had an open-air, rooftop observation deck open to the public. A Marriott Flight Kitchen was established at the west end of the airport to prepare and cater meals for airline flights. In 1965, ABQ saw a total of 289,000 enplaned passengers on 47 flights per day. TWA was operating all its flights with jets by this time, and within two years, the other three airlines would introduce jets as well.

As TWA had a monopoly on every route it flew from Albuquerque, the Civil Aeronautics Board held a special Albuquerque route case in 1969 and issued several new routes to the other three carriers operating at the Sunport. After a US Customs office was opened in 1971, the Municipal Sunport was officially renamed the Albuquerque International Airport. The number of enplaned passengers in 1971 jumped to 594,000 on 70 daily flights. After wide-body jumbo jets were introduced in 1970, the airport built a new west wing addition with one large gate equipped with a jet bridge that opened in 1973. The large TWA hangar, built with the first terminal in 1939, was in the path of the new west wing ramp and was relocated to a point on the south side of the main east-west runway. TWA began using the new west wing gate in 1974 when the carrier introduced a Lockheed L-1011 wide-body aircraft on a flight to Chicago. The west wing gate soon saw more use when traffic began to exceed the capabilities of the main terminal and satellite. Although several new airlines including American, Delta, and Western had applications in with the Civil Aeronautics Board to serve Albuquerque, none were ever granted, and the 1970s only saw growth from the four main carriers and a couple of commuter airlines already serving the airport. That would change dramatically when the airlines were deregulated in late 1978.

This postcard offers an aerial view of the new terminal shortly after it opened in 1965. Notice the satellite gate building at upper right. The airlines were not assigned to specific gates, nor did they have computer equipment at the time, so at first, most flights used the four gates at the main terminal for passenger convenience. None of the gates had jet bridges.

By 1973, a new west wing opened, which included a gate with a jet bridge for wide-body aircraft, as seen in this postcard. The airport was getting much busier by then, prompting more use of the satellite gate building.

This is a view of the Great Hall on the upper level of the terminal in the 1970s. Except for the shops, this portion of the building is much the same today as it was then.

The new terminal had a rooftop observation deck, seen here on the left. Open-air observation areas were very popular for visitors and were constructed at many airports around the world. Today, most viewing areas are enclosed or located away from the terminal.

ALBUQUERQUE
INTERNATIONAL
AIRPORT

A brief history of the
development of the
Albuquerque International
Airport

CONTINENTAL AIRLINES

TWA

TEXAS
INTERNATIONAL
AIRLINES, INC.

FRONTIER AIRLINES

PRESENTED FOR YOUR CONVENIENCE BY
THE CITY OF ALBUQUERQUE AVIATION DEPARTMENT

Brochures were printed and distributed by the Aviation Department in the early 1970s with facts and history on the Albuquerque International Airport. Note the logos of the four airlines serving the airport.

An 18-story Fred Harvey Hotel was constructed in 1973 within a short walk of the terminal. This hotel is most convenient for airline crew layovers. First called the Airport Marina Hotel, ownership has changed several times. It has been a Sheraton since the mid-2010s.

The TWA Boeing 707-131 was one of the first commercial jets to serve ABQ and is seen here landing on the north-south runway in 1969. TWA also had a longer model of the aircraft, the 707-331B Intercontinental, which was used primarily on overseas trips but also flew some domestic flights through ABQ. The 707s continued to serve TWA and ABQ until 1983. (Bob Polaneczky.)

TWA operated Convair 880s on most flights in the late 1960s; however, the aircraft consumed a tremendous amount of fuel and held less than 100 passengers. The Convair 880 was quickly grounded when fuel prices escalated and shortages occurred during the Arab Oil Embargo in 1973.

A TWA Boeing 727-200 is seen here landing on the north-south runway. This stretched version of the 727 with seating for 146 passengers was introduced in the late 1960s and would serve TWA at ABQ for over 30 years. The 727s and the 707s were the two most-operated jet aircraft at ABQ through the 1970s and early 1980s. (Bob Polaneczky.)

On May 1, 1974, TWA introduced the first (and so far only) regularly scheduled commercial wide-body jet service to Albuquerque with the Lockheed L-1011 TriStar. The aircraft flew on one daily flight to Chicago. The jumbo jet service was discontinued in early 1975 but returned in 1982 and continued to serve ABQ for another 10 years. The L-1011 was first configured to hold 206 passengers but later modified to accommodate 275.

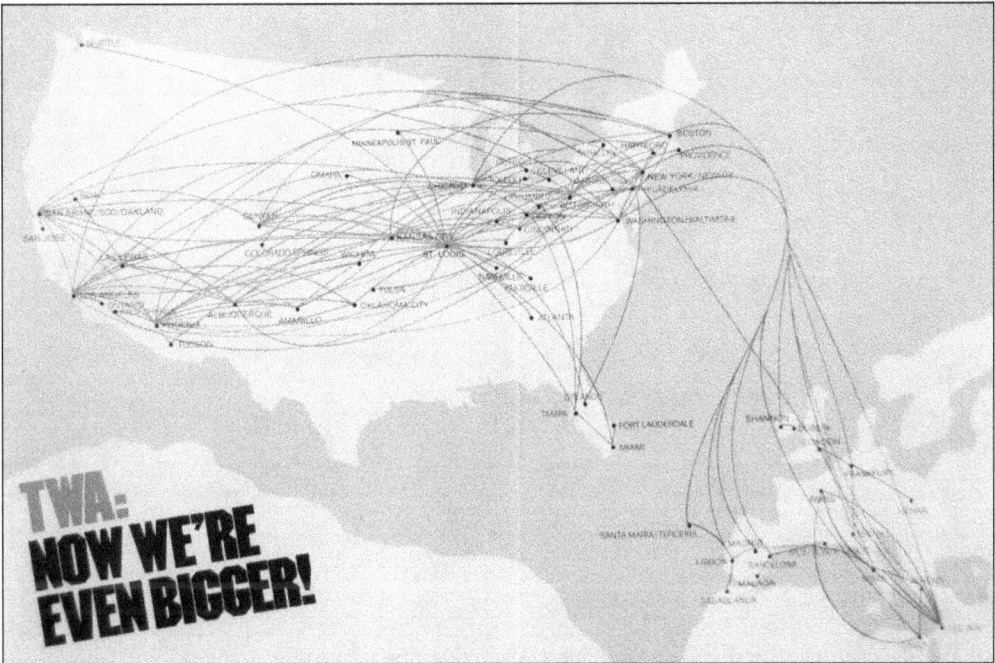

In 1979, TWA tried creating a mini-hub at Albuquerque, adding more routes, including a nonstop flight to New York's John F. Kennedy International Airport (JFK) as shown on this route map from a TWA timetable in 1979. The mini-hub operation grew to a total of 21 flights per day but was scaled back later that same year.

Continental began flying Vickers Viscounts to Albuquerque in 1959 and was operating all flights with Viscounts from late 1963 until early 1966, including this aircraft seen at the new terminal.

In 1966, Continental returned jet service to Albuquerque with the Douglas DC-9. The DC-9s quickly replaced the Viscounts and were used on nearly all flights until late 1969. This DC-9-15 is seen taking off southbound on the north-south runway. The north-south runway (17-35) was only used when needed, as it caused many noise complaints from residents living directly to the north. The runway was closed and removed during the 2010s. (Bob Polaneczky.)

Continental began operating Boeing 727-200s at ABQ in 1969, which replaced all of the smaller DC-9s by 1974. A few of the shorter 727-100s also worked their way through ABQ, and all flights were operated with 727s until 1982. (Jon Proctor.)

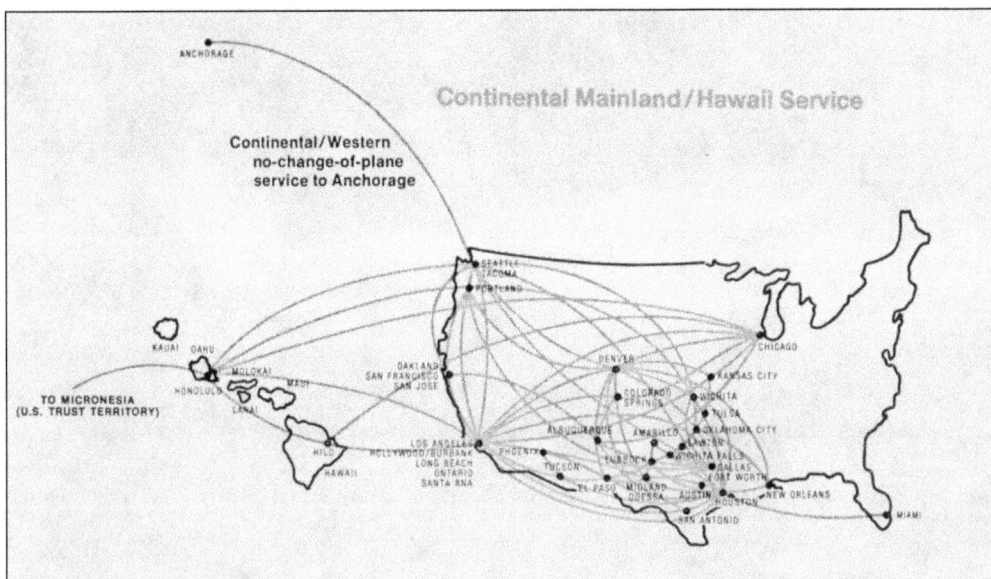

Continental added new nonstop flights from Albuquerque to Chicago, San Francisco, and San Antonio in 1969, as shown on the carrier's route map from an early 1970s timetable. Continental was now operating nonstop to eight cities and reached a peak of 24 departing flights per day in the summer of 1977.

Beginning in 1964, Frontier Airlines upgraded its fleet of Convair 340s with turbo-prop engines, designating the 50-seat aircraft the Convair 580, as shown here. The upgrades were completed by 1966, at which time all of the older DC-3s were retired. (Michael Bernhard.)

Frontier began jet service to Albuquerque in 1967 with the Boeing 727-100 on flights from Denver, El Paso, Tucson, and Phoenix. The stretched 727-200 (pictured) was also added to Frontier's fleet a year later. The 727s were soon replaced with more fuel-efficient Boeing 737s by 1970.

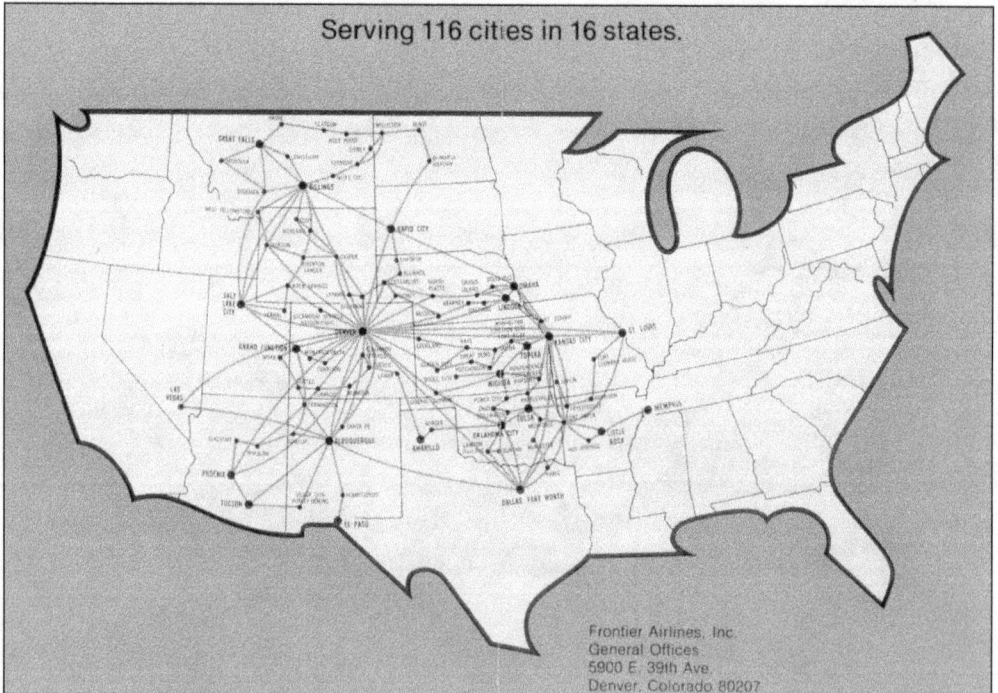

Serving 116 cities in 16 states.

Frontier Airlines, Inc.
General Offices
5900 E. 39th Ave.
Denver, Colorado 80207

Frontier's route map from a late 1969 timetable shows new routes to Dallas and Las Vegas that were awarded to the carrier in the special Albuquerque route case. The routes were flown with newly acquired 737s. Frontier's ABQ service peaked in 1973 with 19 flights per day. Service to Santa Fe ended in mid-1972, and the original route to Salt Lake City, operating with a Convair 580 and still making stops in Farmington and Grand Junction, ended in 1978.

Trans-Texas Airways also began jet service to Albuquerque in 1967 with the 75-seat Douglas DC-9, calling it the Pamper Jet. Initially, the jets made short flights to Santa Fe and Roswell, New Mexico, then onto Midland/Odessa, Dallas, and Houston. The carrier changed its name to Texas International (TI) in 1969 and added a 100-seat stretched version of the DC-9 referred to as the DC-9-30. In early 1970, a new route to Los Angeles was added as well as nonstop flights to Dallas. TI's service to Santa Fe also ended in 1972.

The TI Convair 600 was introduced in 1966. It is pictured here in a livery worn from 1969 through 1972. The aircraft was an updated version of the Convair 240 and continued to serve the smaller cities in New Mexico and Texas until its retirement in 1979. At that time, TI became an all-jet airline, and service to all smaller cities was replaced by commuter airlines. TI did try to service Clovis, Carlsbad, and Hobbs with DC-9s in 1977, but reverted back to the Convair 600s. The jet service to Santa Fe had ended in 1970, but Roswell retained DC-9 jets from ABQ until late 1979. (Bob Polaneczky.)

In 1972, TI changed its branding to more closely resemble the Texas state flag, and several DC-9s were named after a city the carrier serviced. This DC-9-30, N3504T, was christened the *City of Albuquerque*. TI's service at ABQ peaked in 1975 with 13 flights per day. (Jon Proctor.)

Seen here is the August 1, 1979, route map of an all-jet Texas International Airlines. Service to Dallas was changed to the new Dallas/Fort Worth Regional Airport (DFW) in 1974. Flights from Albuquerque to Las Vegas, Salt Lake City, and San Antonio were also added for a short time in the early 1980s. TI merged into Continental Airlines in late 1982.

Bonanza Airlines briefly served Albuquerque on an emergency basis in the summer of 1966, when TWA was shut down due to an extended strike of its machinists. Bonanza provided flights to Phoenix with newly delivered DC-9s, as shown here. The carrier had applied to serve Albuquerque as early as 1959, with a route to Las Vegas, Nevada, that included stops in Gallup, New Mexico, and Grand Canyon, Arizona. Bonanza later merged with two other carriers to become Hughes AirWest, which did receive authority to serve ABQ in late 1978 but did not take it up.

In 1969, Carco was sold to Ross Aviation, which took over the contract for commuter flights to Los Alamos. Ross operated flights every two hours using 18-seat DeHavilland DHC-6 Twin Otters (pictured) and larger 50-seat DeHavilland Dash-7s for heavier loads. The carrier continued service until 1995, when official business to Los Alamos was cut back to the point where the air service was no longer viable.

Other commuter airlines, formally known as air taxis, continued to evolve serving Albuquerque periodically. From 1966 through 1970, Trans Central Airlines operated a route to Denver with several stops along the US highway 85 corridor (now Interstate 25). This route nearly mirrored the route to Denver that Continental operated in the early 1950s. Trans Central used Cessna 402 aircraft.

After Frontier and Texas International suspended service to Santa Fe in 1972, the Santa Fe Airline Company was established, providing commuter flights to and from Albuquerque from 1973 through 1974 using a single-engine Cessna 206. At that time, many passengers flew the short 60-mile trip between the two cities. Service to Taos, New Mexico, was also provided.

Mountain Air provided service on an Albuquerque–Santa Fe–Denver route during 1974 and 1975. A twin-engine Cessna 402 was used, as shown here. Service to Taos and Raton, New Mexico, was also briefly added to the route to Denver. In 1977 and 1978, another carrier, Trans Western Airlines, operated the Albuquerque–Santa Fe–Denver route using a Beech 18 aircraft.

Roswell Airlines provided commuter flights to Roswell and other southeastern New Mexico cities from 1975 through 1978. This photograph is of a model of the airline's Piper Seneca aircraft in the Cavalcade of Wings display in the airport terminal. (Harry Davidson.)

One of the larger and longer lasting commuters was Zia Airlines, which flew from 1974 to 1980 serving nine cities around New Mexico and Colorado from a hub in Albuquerque. The carrier began using Cessna 206 and 402 aircraft and later upgraded to larger Handley-Page Jetstreams, one of which is shown here. Unfortunately, the used Jetstreams had many mechanical issues, ultimately leading to the airline's demise. After Zia's service ended, Stahmann Farms of Las Cruces started an airline with a Las Cruces–Albuquerque–Santa Fe route, Zia's initial and backbone route. Stahmann Farms service only lasted for a few months in late 1980.

Crown Airlines started in 1977 with flights from Albuquerque to Clovis and Lubbock. The carrier expanded to Roswell, Carlsbad, and Hobbs in 1979 after Texas International discontinued service to each city. Crown soon faced competition with other commuters on its routes and shut down in 1980. The carrier used Cessna 402 (pictured) and Piper Navajo aircraft.

Federal Express began operating in 1973 and soon came to Albuquerque, offering overnight package delivery using a Dassault Falcon 20 aircraft, pictured here. FedEx upgraded to much larger 727 aircraft in the 1980s.

At 2:00 a.m. on the morning of November 27, 1971, TWA flight 106 had departed Albuquerque for a flight to Chicago but was hijacked to Cuba. The three hijackers were on the run, having murdered a New Mexico state police officer. They crossed the airport tarmac, entering the Boeing 727 through an aft stairwell (see page 46). The aircraft made a fuel stop in Tampa, Florida, where all passengers were released (pictured here) then continued to Havana, Cuba. The hijackers were apprehended but never returned to the United States. Less than five months later, a Frontier flight destined from Albuquerque to Tucson was hijacked to Los Angeles. As airline hijackings were becoming all too frequent around the world, passenger and carry-on baggage screening was implemented in early 1973.

On November 3, 1973, this National Airlines Douglas DC-10 jumbo jet suffered an engine explosion on a flight from Houston to Las Vegas while cruising over west-central New Mexico. Shrapnel from the engine shattered a window, causing decompression of the aircraft and pulling one passenger out to his death. The DC-10 was able to make an emergency landing at ABQ with no further injuries.

One of the first Boeing 747s to land at ABQ was a Korean Airlines charter flight in 1979. The 747 was the largest of the jumbo jets and is known as the "Queen of the Skies." The 747 used for the charter, like the one shown here, flew to Anchorage, Alaska, and then on to Seoul, Korea.

Five

DEREGULATION BRINGS MANY NEW AIRLINES

1979–1992

On October 24, 1978, Pres. Jimmy Carter signed the Airline Deregulation Act. Up until then, many new airlines had been applying to the Civil Aeronautics Board to serve Albuquerque, but none were ever approved. The airport was up to 90 flights per day, and now, new airlines were nearly free to begin service at will. From 1979 to 1992, thirteen new major airlines began service to Albuquerque, and new routes to major hub cities such as Atlanta, Minneapolis, and Pittsburgh came with them. Deregulation also meant that airlines could now drop routes that no longer fit into their system. Such was the case with Continental Airlines and its Albuquerque-Chicago and Dallas/Fort Worth (DFW) routes. Continental did not have hubs in either Chicago or DFW, and the routes were no longer beneficial to them after American Airlines, which operates large hubs at both airports, began servicing the routes very soon after the deregulation act was signed. TWA had been maintaining one flight a day in each direction along its original mainline route between Los Angeles and New York that made stops in Albuquerque, Amarillo, Wichita, and Chicago. This "milk run" route also ended as TWA, like most other carriers, was developing a hub and spoke route structure using St. Louis as its major hub. There are some exceptions, such as that no city could be left without any air service, and this was the case with most of the smaller cities in New Mexico that were served by Frontier and Texas International. Other airlines had to be found to serve these cities before the designated carrier could end service, but no other local service airlines were willing to pick them up. Smaller commuter airlines were the answer to this problem, and deregulation saw many new commuters evolve at a rapid pace eager to service the smaller cities and link them to New Mexico's largest city. In many cases, these commuter airlines were subsidized by the government in a program known as Essential Air Service, or EAS. By 1987, the commuters alone flew over 70 flights per day at ABQ.

Along with all the new airlines came growing pains. Airlines had to share ticket counters and aircraft had to double up on gates. Three more gates were added to the west wing in 1980; however, the terminal building was still way outgrown, and by the mid-1980s, a massive expansion was desperately needed.

American Airlines was the first new carrier to begin service to Albuquerque after deregulation. American began flights on January 20, 1979, with Boeing 727s to Dallas/Fort Worth and San Francisco; however, the San Francisco flight was quickly discontinued. New flights to Chicago were added one year later, followed by service to El Paso. This photograph shows a Boeing 727-200 with a shorter 727-100 in the background, both parked at west wing gates.

Eastern Airlines was the second new major carrier beginning service in late 1979 but the first to begin a new route, in which it linked Albuquerque with its main hub in Atlanta. Eastern used 727s (a -200 model is shown here parked at the satellite building). The carrier also operated flights to Dallas/Fort Worth, Phoenix, and El Paso in the early 1980s, and for a brief time in 1983, Eastern flew a brand-new Boeing 757 on a flight to Atlanta. The carrier later added flights to Kansas City and Tucson but discontinued all service in 1988 and went out of business three years later.

Southwest Airlines began Albuquerque service on April 3, 1980, with four daily flights to Dallas Love Field. The carrier soon added flights to El Paso, and as TWA and Continental were discontinuing routes, Southwest quickly expanded, adding new service to cities all over the Southwest. The airline became the busiest carrier at ABQ within only two years and has always operated Boeing 737s, with the initial -200 version shown here. For a short time in 1984 and 1985, Southwest operated 727-200s while awaiting delivery of new 737-300s, which were much more powerful and fuel efficient. (Brad Kostelny.)

United Airlines started flights to its Denver hub on June 15, 1982, and soon added service to Chicago, San Francisco, and El Paso. Boeing 727-100s and -200s, along with 737-200s, were first used. Pictured here is a 727-200. New 737-300s were introduced in 1988.

Western Airlines returned to Albuquerque on October 25, 1981, after being the first airline to serve the city in 1929 as Western Air Express. The carrier first used 727-200s (pictured) on routes to Las Vegas, San Francisco, and Houston and later added 737-200s. Service to Phoenix and El Paso was soon added as well. In 1982, Western began building major hub operations at Salt Lake City and Los Angeles, adding flights to ABQ as one of its spoke cities. Western had been applying to return to Albuquerque as early as 1945 with a route to Salt Lake City, which initially included stops in Durango and Grand Junction, Colorado. (Bruce Drum.)

Delta Air Lines began Albuquerque service on February 15, 1983, with flights to its Dallas/Fort Worth hub, and soon added flights to Atlanta. The carrier also first used 727-200s, pictured here, with 737-200s and -300s soon added. Delta and Western merged in 1987, retaining the Delta brand.

Pacific Southwest Airlines, or PSA, began flights from Albuquerque to Los Angeles and San Francisco in 1983, using new McDonnell Douglas MD-80s (pictured) and Boeing 727-200s. The carrier was prompted to serve ABQ as TWA had discontinued its service to Los Angeles. PSA's service was suspended for a period in 1985 and 1986 but returned and continued until the carrier merged into USAir in 1988.

Wien Air Alaska made a surprising appearance in Albuquerque for three months in the spring of 1984. The carrier flew a 727-200 on a flight to Denver and a 737-200 (pictured) on a flight to Oakland, California. Both flights continued on to Seattle and Anchorage. Wien went out of business later that year. (Bruce Drum.)

America West Airlines was a new carrier that began operations in the summer of 1983 with a hub in Phoenix. It started flights to Albuquerque later that year, using 737-200s (pictured). Service was also added to Oklahoma City, Tulsa, and Wichita, but those routes were soon discontinued. Larger Boeing 737-300s were added in 1985, and new routes to Austin, Durango, and El Paso were briefly flown. A late-night flight to Las Vegas also began that was maintained through the 1990s. (Bruce Drum.)

Braniff Airways was a legacy carrier in the United States dating to 1928. The carrier declared bankruptcy and shut down in 1982 but reemerged two years later, building a hub in Kansas City. The new Braniff came to Albuquerque in 1988 with flights to Kansas City and Tucson using 727-200s (pictured) and 737-200s. Service to ABQ lasted about a year and a half, and the new Braniff shut down in late 1989.

In 1988, PSA merged into USAir, which began USAir's service to Albuquerque. PSA's former flights to Los Angeles were soon discontinued, and USAir began new nonstop flights to its major hub in Pittsburgh. Boeing 737-300s and -400s (pictured) were mainly used, and a 757 made a brief appearance in early 1995. For a short time, USAir also operated flights to Tucson, a flight to Philadelphia with a stop in Kansas City, and a flight to Charlotte with a stop in Denver. All USAir service to Albuquerque was discontinued in 1997, but would return 10 years later.

Pan American World Airways was long the largest and, as it claimed, "most experienced" airline in the world. Pan Am served Albuquerque with a single flight to New York's JFK airport by way of Dallas/Fort Worth during the winter of 1989–1990. A 727-200 was used, and the service to ABQ was the shortest of any major airline, lasting only 54 days. Pan Am was struggling financially at that time and shut down in late 1991.

After nearly 14 years since airline deregulation was passed, the long-awaited Northwest Airlines began flights to Minneapolis/St. Paul on October 1, 1992. Service first started using DC-9-30 aircraft and then upgraded to 727-200s (pictured).

A number of new commuter airlines also came to ABQ with airline deregulation. The first was Air Midwest beginning on March 1, 1979, taking over the former routes of Frontier and Texas International from Albuquerque to seven smaller cities in New Mexico. Air Midwest used 17-seat Swearingen Metroliners and operated as many as 18 daily flights from Albuquerque. Service continued until early 1986. (Jon Jamieson.)

Aspen Airways also began ABQ service on March 1, 1979, with Convair 580 flights to Farmington that continued on to Durango. The service only lasted a few months; however, Aspen continued to serve Farmington and Durango from Denver and became a United Express feeder carrier in 1986.

In 1979, Desert Airlines operated eight-seat Piper Navajos to Gallup and on to Phoenix, with stops in Winslow and Flagstaff, Arizona. Service ended in early 1980.

Sun West Airlines began operations in 1980 with flights to Gallup, Farmington, and Durango. The Gallup flights would continue on to Winslow or Flagstaff, Arizona, then on to Phoenix much like the previous carrier, Desert Airlines. Sun West first used Piper Navajos (pictured), then upgraded to 14-seat Beech C99s in 1983. Nonstop service to Tucson was also briefly operated in 1983, but the carrier shut down two years later.

Mesa Airlines began operations in 1980 using a single-engine Piper Saratoga on a route from Albuquerque to Farmington. Mesa grew quickly, and by 1987, was serving 14 communities throughout New Mexico plus several more cities in surrounding states. Mesa became by far the largest commuter airline in New Mexico, operating as many as 47 departing flights per day at its Albuquerque hub. The carrier received a government subsidy on many of its routes. Mesa upgraded its aircraft fleet with Piper Navajos in 1981 followed by Beech C99s in 1983 (above), 19-seat Beech 1900Cs in 1985 (below), and Beech 1300s in 1988. Two 9-seat Cessna Caravans were operated from 1987 through 1991 for new service to very small cities.

A new Pioneer Airlines (no relation to the previous Pioneer of the 1940s and 1950s) served Albuquerque in 1982 and 1983 with flights to Farmington, Durango, Santa Fe, and Colorado Springs. The carrier mainly flew Swearingen Metroliner aircraft, one of which is pictured here at the Santa Fe airport.

Trans-Colorado Airlines provided commuter service to Durango and Colorado Springs beginning in late 1983 using Swearingen Metroliners (above). At first, the Durango flights continued on to Gunnison, Colorado. The carrier later added service to Farmington, Roswell, and Carlsbad and became a Continental Express feeder carrier in mid-1986 (below). A 50-seat Convair 580 was briefly used in April 1987 for Continental Express service to Farmington and Tucson. Continental Airlines did not have a hub at ABQ, and the Continental Express operation was short-lived, ending in mid-1987.

JetAire began operations in early 1985 with a single 16-seat Handley-Page Jetstream on a route between Albuquerque and Las Cruces. The carrier tried serving Alamogordo and other cities with the one aircraft as well and never put any additional aircraft into service. Alamogordo and Las Cruces were previously served by Airways of New Mexico from 1981 until that carrier shut down in mid-1985. JetAire also shut down after one year of operation.

StatesWest Airlines operated a daily flight to Tucson and a weekend flight to Phoenix for a short time in the fall of 1987. StatesWest used a British Aerospace Jetstream 31, an advanced version of the Handley-Page Jetstream.

Air Ruidoso operated in 1987 and 1988, using a Piper Navajo Chieftain on flights to Ruidoso, New Mexico. Air Ruidoso was the only airline providing service to its hometown of Ruidoso; however, its operating certificate was revoked, causing it to shut down.

Territorial Airlines also made an attempt to serve communities that had lost air service. For a short time in the summer of 1990, the carrier connected Albuquerque to Las Vegas and Raton, New Mexico, using a Piper Navajo Chieftain. The airline was run from the shop of the Santa Fe Cookie Company.

Aspen Airways returned to ABQ for the winter of 1989–1990, operating as United Express. The carrier was primarily providing feeder flights for United Airlines in Denver but spun off one flight from Durango to Albuquerque for the ski season that year. Convair 580s were still being used, and the 38-year-old carrier shut down at the end of that ski season, being sold mostly to Mesa Airlines.

Pictured here is an aerial view of the terminal in 1985. Note the west wing on the left, now featuring four gates with jet bridges. Southwest's two gates on the right side of the main terminal were fitted with three jet bridges that went from ground level up to the plane.

The TWA Lockheed L-1011 wide-body returned to ABQ in 1982 on a flight from St. Louis. At times, a Boeing 767 wide-body was used in place of the L-1011, and in the summer of 1987, two L-1011 flights were operated. From 1979 through 1985, TWA had downsized its ABQ operation from 21 flights per day serving 12 cities to four flights per day, all to St. Louis. This paint scheme on the L-1011, which included double red stripes, was adopted in the mid-1970s and was similar to the livery used by the carrier in the 1950s.

TWA operated an Ambassador's Club for its premier customers through the 1980s and 1990s with traditional Southwestern architecture and décor. Today, the room is known as the Sandia Vista room and is available for small meetings and conferences. It is still dedicated to TWA and includes a memorial to the crash of flight 260 in 1955 (see page 44).

Continental merged Texas International Airlines into its operation in late 1982 but declared bankruptcy and completely shut down one year later. The carrier soon reorganized and returned service to ABQ by mid-1984 with flights to Denver and Houston. Service was later added back to El Paso, and a new flight to Las Vegas operated into the late 1980s. New Boeing 737-300s with more powerful and fuel-efficient engines, like the one seen here, were added to replace the aging 727s.

Frontier Airlines became an all-jet airline in 1982 after the last of its Convair 580s was retired and service to most of its smaller cities was taken over by commuter airlines. New routes were added from Albuquerque to several cities in Mexico as well as to Midland/Odessa, Texas. Frontier was now serving ABQ mostly with 737-200s (pictured) and an occasional MD-80 in a new paint scheme with different shades of red and orange stripes. The airline ceased all operations on August 24, 1986, and most of its assets were later acquired by Continental.

A new general aviation complex was constructed in a pentagon shape on the opposite (south) side of the main east-west runway in the mid-1980s. This is the new home for Cutter (lower center) as well as Atlantic Aviation and other fixed based operators (FBOs), which service general aviation. Most charter flights that cannot be conducted at the main terminal are handled here. Other FBOs that served the Sunport were Mueller Aero Service and WesternAir Inc.

The larger building on the left is the original airfreight warehouse, built in the mid-1970s. Freight traffic growth was nearly as impressive as passenger traffic in the 1980s, and a new and much larger airfreight facility was built on the southwest corner of the airfield in 1992. The building on the right is the original terminal of 1939, with the original hangar directly above it.

UPS began airfreight services in 1980, operating flights from Albuquerque to its main hub in Louisville, Kentucky. Pictured here is a stretch Douglas DC-8-73. The company upgraded its fleet with wide-body Boeing 767-300s by the early 1990s.

From 1984 through 1996, UPS also had its own feeder flights from smaller cities around New Mexico. This aircraft, a Swearingen Metro Expeditor, was contracted through Merlin Express and painted with UPS branding.

Airborne Express operated two versions of the Douglas DC-9 to ABQ: the -31 and the slightly longer -41 (pictured) with cargo flights from Wilmington, Ohio. (Brad Kostelny.)

Airborne Express was sold to DHL in 2003, which continued using the DC-9-41 aircraft and served ABQ from Wilmington, Ohio, until 2008. DHL now contracts with a small carrier, Ameriflight, which operates a Beech 99 aircraft to Phoenix that connects with large DHL aircraft there.

Emery Worldwide served ABQ with air cargo flights to its hub in Dayton, Ohio. Boeing 707s, 727s, and this stretch DC-8-63 were used. The carrier was shut down in 2001.

Burlington Northern Air Freight Inc. began operations in 1972 with offices in Irvine, California, and Toledo, Ohio. The name was changed to Burlington Air Express in 1986 and again to BAX Global in 1997. The carrier provided service at ABQ with Douglas DC-8s and this Boeing 727-200 until it was shut down in 2011.

Evergreen International served ABQ with this Douglas DC-9-15F during the 1980s and 1990s. Many other smaller freight carriers have also served ABQ, mostly with piston and turboprop aircraft.

Six

TERMINAL EXPANSION
1990s

By the mid-1980s, ABQ was bursting at the seams once again. A massive $120 million expansion of the current terminal took place from 1987 through 1989, adding a second level to the front of the building that provided separate levels for departing and arriving passengers. The small, four-gate satellite building was replaced with two concourses, A and B, providing a total of 19 new gates, each with jet bridges. An aboveground connector building was erected over the area of the underground tunnel, and the four gates at the main terminal were converted to commuter airline gates. The tunnel, which has walls decorated with Southwestern tile art, was preserved; however, it is not accessible to the public. In all, the terminal now had 22 gates with jet bridges plus four commuter gates. A four-level parking garage was constructed in front of the terminal where only ground level parking previously existed, and in 1997, a new primary access road named Sunport Boulevard was built linking the airport directly to Interstate 25.

Many major carriers across the country began discontinuing use of wide-body jets on domestic routes in the 1990s, and TWA, in turn, ended the L-1011 flights to ABQ in 1992. The airport was officially renamed the Albuquerque International Sunport in 1994, bringing back the "Sunport" name the facility held prior to 1971. A new development in this decade was the introduction of the regional jet, or RJ, seating 50 passengers. Delta Connection, operated by SkyWest Airlines on behalf of Delta, was the first to introduce an RJ to Albuquerque, with flights to Delta's Salt Lake City hub beginning in 1995. ABQ did lose service by one major carrier, however. USAir, which had just changed its name to US Airways, discontinued all service in 1997, as it was only flying to Pittsburgh at the time and was downsizing that airport as a major hub. Overall, the 1990s were booming at ABQ, and amongst all carriers at the Sunport, there were as many as 164 commercial airline departures per day, carrying over five million passengers per year.

Other major areas of growth that took place on the airport grounds included an all-new cargo facility that opened in 1992 near the new general aviation area, replacing the former facility near the old terminal. A new post office was built just west of the old terminal building, and a new and much taller control tower was erected on the grounds of Kirtland Air Force Base, which is closer to the terminal, providing controllers with much clearer views of the terminal ramp. All of these new facilities have produced vast improvements in the airport's operation.

This postcard shows an overhead view of the newly expanded terminal with 22 gates, all equipped with jet bridges, and four commuter gates after completion in 1989. The top level of the parking garage was later equipped with solar panels, which now supply much of the power to the Sunport.

ALBUQUERQUE INTERNATIONAL AIRPORT

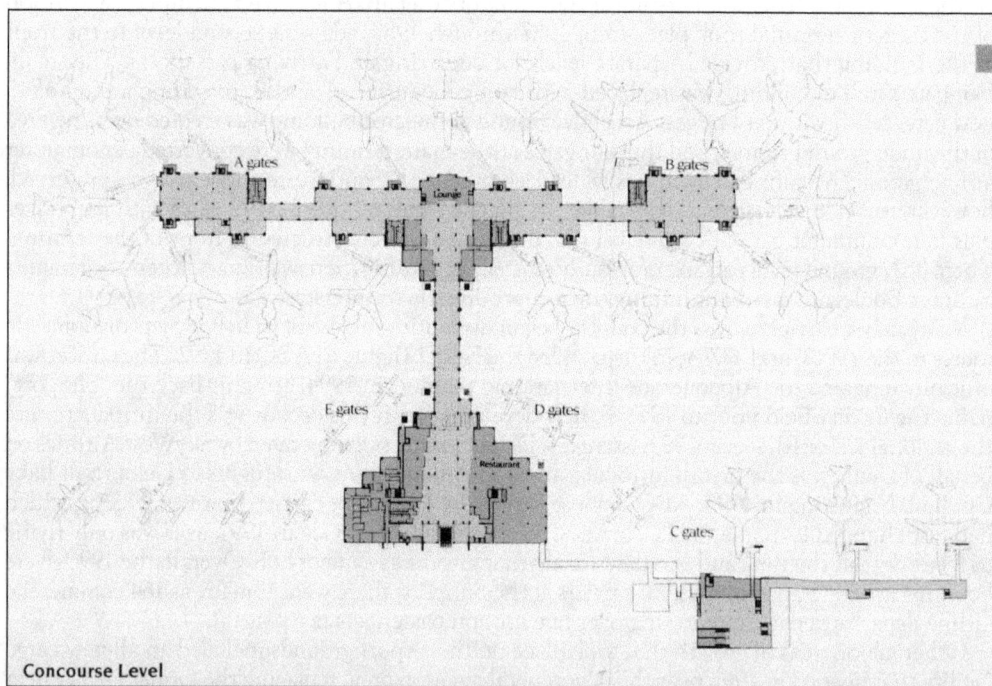

Concourse Level

This diagram shows the layout of the terminal's upper level and all the new gates in 1989. In 1996, the A concourse was lengthened with four more gates, and the C concourse was later decommissioned except for the first gate, which handles international arrivals. Commuter airlines used the D and E gates; however, the D gates were also decommissioned in the mid-2000s. There have been many times when every gate has been in use. At night, several aircraft are pushed back away from the gates to make room for more planes.

The Great Hall in the center of the terminal was preserved and renovated during the expansion. An actual 1914 Ingram Foster biplane is on display in the front and center of this photograph. Around the island at the base of the biplane are several historical photographs of aviation in Albuquerque, many of which are also included in this book.

A statue titled *Dream of Flight* was installed in the food court area at the junction of the A and B concourses. The level above and behind the statue is a fully enclosed observation lounge that was added on in the late 1990s.

TWA began operating the MD-80 aircraft in 1984, which replaced the 727s and the L-1011 by the mid-1990s. This MD-80 wears the livery that TWA adopted in 1995.

American started flying MD-80s to ABQ in 1985 and replaced all 727s by the mid-1990s. Nearly all mainline flights were then operated with MD-80s for the next two decades, with up to 12 flights per day. Occasionally, a Boeing 757 came through on select flights during the 1990s. The MD-80 shown here was still operating in 2019, but the final retirement of the fleet is very near.

Continental discontinued its hub operation at Denver in 1994 and reduced its service at ABQ to only five daily flights to Houston. The carrier adopted this new look in 1991 and added other versions of the 737, including the shorter -500 model seen here.

United discontinued its flights to Chicago, El Paso, and San Francisco in the late 1980s and only operated flights to its Denver hub through the 1990s. The carrier began flying new Boeing 737-500 and 757 aircraft on up to nine flights per day to Denver with as many as four on the larger 757s. At the end of the 1990s, United introduced the Airbus A319, seen here wearing the "Battleship Grey" livery. Larger Airbus A320 aircraft were introduced two years later.

In 1995, Delta introduced new Delta Connection service to ABQ with regional jets (RJs). Fifty-seat Canadair CRJ-200s were operated by SkyWest Airlines, seen here, with flights to Salt Lake City and later to Dallas/Fort Worth. Meanwhile, Delta added new service to its Cincinnati hub as well as to Colorado Springs and Tucson. New aircraft also arrived, including Boeing 737-800s, 757s, and MD-88s. Delta was the second largest carrier at ABQ through the 1990s, operating up to 15 daily flights.

America West introduced a larger Boeing 757 on one of its Phoenix flights during the late 1990s, shown here in a new livery adopted in 1996. Airbus A319 and A320 aircraft were also introduced in the 1990s.

A new Frontier Airlines evolved in the summer of 1994, establishing a hub in Denver and beginning a Denver–Albuquerque–El Paso route later that year using 737-200s. Newer 737-300s were added within a few years, and the carrier completely switched to operating Airbus aircraft (A318s, A319s, and A320s) by the early 2000s. The new Frontier has a unique concept of applying a decal of a different type of wildlife on the tail of each of its aircraft. This was the first 737-200, featuring Clover the fawn.

Reno Air, another new carrier, began flights to Los Angeles and San Jose, California, in 1995 using MD-80 and shorter MD-87 (pictured) aircraft. The carrier briefly experimented with flights to Reno and Colorado Springs in 1996, followed by a flight to Durango during the 1996–1997 ski season. In 1997, the flights to Los Angeles were discontinued, and three daily flights to Las Vegas were initiated. All service to Albuquerque ended in 1998, and the carrier merged into American Airlines one year later.

By the mid-1990s, Southwest had outgrown its facilities in the A concourse, and the building was lengthened, adding four more gates. Southwest had created a small hub at ABQ and grew with as many as 66 departing flights per day. Four Southwest aircraft can be seen here, and the carrier used five more gates on the other side of the concourse as well. All of the aircraft shown here are next-generation Boeing 737-700s first introduced in 1998.

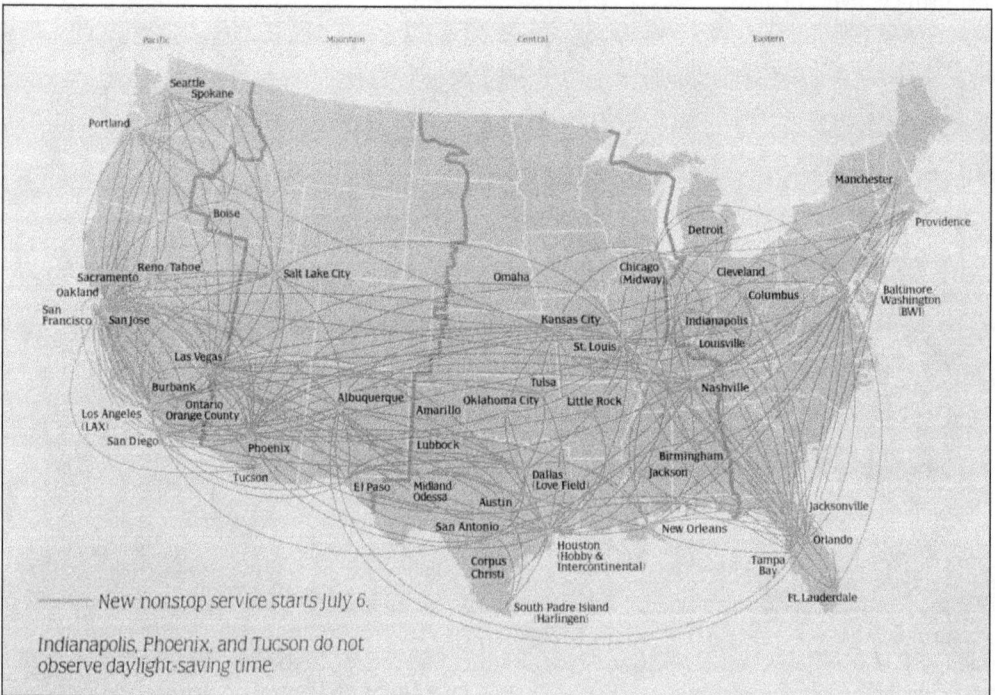

New nonstop service starts July 6.

Indianapolis, Phoenix, and Tucson do not observe daylight-saving time.

Southwest's route map from 1998 shows flights from Albuquerque to 21 cities nationwide. Southwest was now operating to all but three cities that both TWA and Continental had once served with jets from Albuquerque. A reservations office was also opened near the Sunport.

Most commuter airlines at ABQ did not make it past the 1980s, but Mesa Airlines prevailed by dominating the market in the smaller cities of New Mexico. The carrier ultimately settled on the 19-seat Beechcraft 1900D (the "D" referring to it having a standup cabin), six of which can be seen here parked at the E gates of the terminal on a typical day in the 1990s. For a short while in 1992, Mesa operated a 30-seat Embraer Brasilia on some of its hourly flights to Farmington. By the end of the decade, however, high-flying Mesa would begin to descend.

Mesa's route map from its July 16, 1990, timetable shows the extensive route structure from its Albuquerque hub. Flights to Taos and Ruidoso were flown with a single-engine Cessna 208 Caravan aircraft. Service to Los Alamos was briefly operated in 1997.

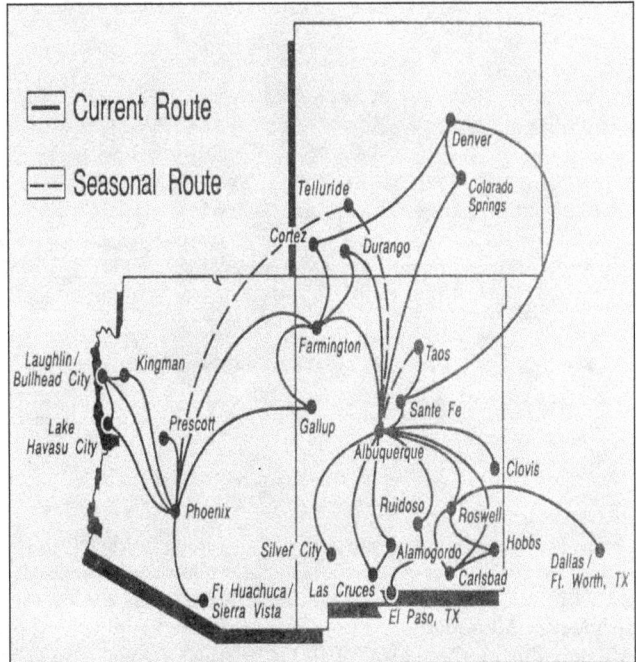

Arizona Airways began flights to Tucson in 1993 using a 13-seat Beech 1300 aircraft, pictured here. Tucson was a small hub for Arizona Airways, and the carrier provided connecting flights to several cities in northern Mexico that were otherwise hard to reach from Albuquerque. Arizona Airways later upgraded to Beech 1900C aircraft and was merged into Great Lakes Airlines in 1996. Great Lakes continued serving the route to Tucson for a short time before ending service in mid-1997.

AeroLitoral, a feeder airline for AeroMexico, was the first international carrier to begin regular service to Albuquerque. The airline operated flights to Ciudad Juarez then on to Chihuahua, Mexico, during the winter of 1993–1994 using Swearingen Metroliners.

Peacock Air, a division of Merlin Express, operated a Swearingen Metroliner on the Albuquerque–Los Alamos route during the latter half of 1995 after Ross Aviation ended its service. For a very short time in December 1995, the carrier flew an Albuquerque–Flagstaff–Bullhead City/Laughlin, Nevada, roundtrip flight.

Mountain Air Express (MAX) was a feeder carrier for Western Pacific Airlines, an upstart airline in the 1990s with a hub in Colorado Springs. The carrier switched its hub to Denver in 1997 and began feeder flights with MAX to Albuquerque and Santa Fe. For added revenue, Western Pacific would paint its aircraft with advertising for different companies, locales, and events. This MAX Dornier 328 prop aircraft promotes Cheyenne Frontier Days, which occurs during July of each year in Cheyenne, Wyoming. The ABQ service was short-lived, ending later in 1997, and Western Pacific went out of business in early 1998.

Many charter airlines have served Albuquerque. Two of the regulars during the 1990s were Great American and Casino Express, which operated casino junket flights to Wendover and Elko, Nevada. Great American flew the DC-9 at left, and Casino Express the 737-200 at right.

American Trans Air also operated frequent charters using this 727-200 and several other aircraft, including a stretch 757-300.

At least three Mexican charter airlines were seen at ABQ during the 1990s. Pictured here is an Aviacsa 727-200, which operated public charter flights to Mazatlan, Mexico, during spring break in 1996.

Seven

REGIONAL JETS

2000s

After the tragic events of September 11, 2001, air traffic around the nation tumbled, and ABQ was no exception. Many carriers dropped flights and grounded older aircraft, notably the Boeing 727. Due to increased security, the connector hallway from the main terminal to the A and B concourses was greatly expanded to provide much needed additional space for the security checkpoint. This expansion brought the terminal up to 600,000 square feet of operating space. Two of the west wing C gates became structurally unstable, causing them to be condemned and ultimately demolished. The original west wing gate, built in 1973, still houses US Customs and is used for arriving international flights from Mexico. As this gate no longer has security screening, aircraft must then be repositioned to another gate within the secure area for departure.

Contract airlines operating regional jets gained much momentum at ABQ starting in 2002, as most of the other carriers followed Delta by beginning RJ flights one after another. American Eagle, Continental Express, United Express, America West Express, US Airways Express, Frontier Jet Express, Northwest Airlink, and AeroMexico Connect all began service with RJs on behalf of their major carriers. Larger RJs soon came on the scene, accommodating up to 86 passengers. The aircraft became so popular that there were times when all flights operated by a specific airline were flown by contract carriers operating RJs.

Commuter airline traffic took a huge hit beginning in the late 1990s, when stricter rules were imposed on the industry, which saw increased costs that had to be passed on to the customers by means of higher fares. Mesa Airlines saw a steady decline in traffic and was forced to trim flights until its Albuquerque operation had completely dissolved by the end of 2007. The D commuter gates in the main terminal were closed, as the E gates were more than adequate. ABQ had become less of a hub for the state of New Mexico, as the cities of Clovis, Hobbs, Roswell, and Santa Fe had all landed direct service to the major hubs of Dallas/Fort Worth, Denver, Houston, and Phoenix, mostly with RJs. Major airline traffic had rebounded nicely since 9/11, but by the end of the decade, the economy went into a recession and fuel prices skyrocketed, causing airfares to greatly increase and traffic to tumble once again.

The decade also saw the Sunport begin a program where volunteers can serve as ambassadors who greet and assist passengers. The ambassadors often bring their dogs to help provide comfort and ease to the traveling public.

The new millennium began with the sunset of TWA. American Airlines purchased the ailing carrier, and a full merger of the two companies took place on December 2, 2001. TWA's last arrival into ABQ from St. Louis the day before received a water-cannon salute in honor of the airline's service (above). The flight crew (left) consisted of the captain (second from right), first officer (left of the captain), three female flight attendants, and a male purser on the far left. After the final flight departed for St. Louis, the MD-80 aircraft circled back around and made a traditional final fly-by in salute for providing 72 years of service to the city of Albuquerque (below). American retained service on TWA's sole route to St. Louis for two more years but ultimately discontinued the entire St. Louis hub operation.

American Eagle began service to Albuquerque in 2002 with a single flight to Los Angeles using this 44-seat Embraer-140 RJ. The service ended later that year, but American Eagle returned in 2007, replacing American's flights to Chicago with 70-seat CRJ-700 RJs. Eagle service to Los Angeles returned in 2012.

Frontier began a regional operation in 2003, supplementing its flights to Denver. Mesa, Horizon, and Republic Airlines operated a variety of RJs as Frontier Jet Express. Service to Puerto Vallarta, Mexico, was briefly flown in 2008. Frontier also established its own feeder carrier in 2006, Lynx, which operated 76-seat Bombardier Dash-8-Q400 turboprops on the Albuquerque-Denver route. Seen here is a 99-seat Embraer-190 operated by Republic Airlines featuring Buddy the badger. All Frontier regional and feeder operations were discontinued in 2013.

In 2003, Continental began replacing its flights to Houston with Continental Express 50-seat Embraer-145 RJs operated by ExpressJet, a subsidiary of Continental Airlines. Seasonal weekend flights to Cleveland were also periodically operated by Continental Express. During the annual Albuquerque International Hot Air Balloon Fiesta held in early October, Continental added extra flights and larger aircraft such as Boeing 737-700s, -800s, and -900s and 757s to handle the customer demand. Nonstop flights to Newark were occasionally operated during the 2000s as well.

United Express returned to ABQ in 2003 with RJs supplementing United's flights to Denver. New Express service was soon added to Chicago, Los Angeles, and San Francisco, and Express flights to San Antonio were briefly operated in 2006. Seen here is a United Express CRJ-700 operated by SkyWest Airlines in the "Rising Blue" paint scheme. Other carriers that operated as United Express at ABQ include Chautauqua and Shuttle America Airlines. In 2006, United Airlines began a nonstop flight to Washington Dulles International Airport.

Other Delta Connection carriers began supplementing SkyWest with flights to Salt Lake City beginning in 2005. Shown here is a CRJ-700 operated by Atlantic Southeast Airlines in Delta's new "Colors in Motion" livery. ExpressJet, Mesaba, and Pinnacle Airlines also operated as Delta Connection for brief periods of time.

Northwest replaced its 727s at ABQ with Airbus A319s and A320s in 2001 and supplemented its Minneapolis service with Northwest Airlink flights in 2004 through 2005. Seen here is a Northwest Airlink CRJ-200 operated by Pinnacle Airlines and wearing a new livery for Northwest Airlines.

America West Airlines began its America West Express service on flights to Phoenix in 2002 using a combination of CRJ-200, CRJ-700 (pictured), and CRJ-900 regional jets operated by Mesa Airlines. Mesa had transitioned from a commuter airline to a regional carrier operating all RJs for large airlines. America West merged into US Airways in 2007.

US Airways returned to ABQ in 2007 as a result of the merger with America West. The carrier maintained flights to Phoenix and made a brief run to Charlotte during the summer of 2015. Most service to ABQ was performed by US Airways Express using CRJ-200s and CRJ-900s operated by both Mesa and SkyWest Airlines. Shown here is an 86-seat CRJ-900 flown by Mesa. Both times US Airways served ABQ were due to mergers with carriers already operating at the Sunport.

Rio Grande Air, a commuter airline based in Taos, New Mexico, evolved in 1999 providing service to Los Alamos and Taos using single engine nine-seat Cessna 208 Grand Caravans. The carrier later expanded with flights to Farmington, Durango, Santa Fe, and Ruidoso and also secured a subsidized contract for flights to Alamogordo. As Rio Grande Air was attempting to acquire a larger aircraft type in 2004, its financing did not materialize, causing the carrier to shut down.

Great Plains Airlines, an independent carrier operating regional jets, began service in 2001 with an Albuquerque–Oklahoma City–Tulsa–Nashville route using this 32-seat Fairchild Dornier 328Jet. The carrier later began flights to Austin and Colorado Springs and started a code-share agreement with Rio Grande Air, rather unusual for such a small airline. Great Plains also ended service in 2004.

Great Lakes Airlines (left) returned to ABQ in 2005, replacing Mesa Airlines on its routes to Clovis and Silver City. Great Lakes also served Santa Fe and Alamosa, Colorado, for short times as well, but its traffic continually declined until Albuquerque service ended in 2012. Mesa Airlines (right) discontinued its Albuquerque independent hub operation at the end of 2007 and now serves ABQ with all RJs on behalf of several major carriers. Both aircraft seen here are Beech 1900Ds, a very popular commuter aircraft in the 1990s and 2000s.

Westward Airways of Nebraska came to New Mexico in late 2004 with routes from Albuquerque to Alamogordo, Gallup, Las Cruces, and Taos. The carrier operated Pilatus PC-12 aircraft but had a short life, ending all service in mid-2005.

ExpressJet had been operating solely as Continental Express but began its own independent operation in 2007 by servicing routes that no other carrier was flying. From Albuquerque, ExpressJet flew to Austin, San Antonio, Oklahoma City, Tulsa, Sacramento, and Ontario, California. Unfortunately, fuel prices skyrocketed at this time, making it nearly unprofitable to operate 50-seat regional jets like this Embraer-145. ExpressJet shut down its independent operation a year later but continued flying as Continental Express.

AeroMexico Connect operated by Aerolitoral made a comeback to Albuquerque in 2009 through negotiations between the Mexican government and Bill Richardson, the governor of New Mexico. The carrier operated three flights per week to Chihuahua, Mexico, using an Embraer-145. Although Aerolitoral was subsidized by the governments of both Mexico and New Mexico, the route did not become profitable and ended in early 2010.

New Mexico Airlines, a division of Pacific Wings based in Hawaii, took over the subsidized service to Alamogordo, Carlsbad, and Hobbs in 2007 using a fleet of Cessna 208 Grand Caravans seen here. Service to Roswell was proposed but later canceled, as American Eagle had begun RJ service to Dallas/Fort Worth. Service to Hobbs was discontinued in 2011 when United Express began RJ service from that city to Houston. The Alamogordo flights ended in 2012 when traffic declined to the point where its government subsidy was canceled. Service was briefly operated to Los Alamos and Ruidoso, and flights to Carlsbad were maintained until early 2015, when the carrier was shut down.

Southwest Airlines has a theme of painting an aircraft in the colors of the state flag for states in which they have a large presence. Even though Albuquerque is the only city Southwest serves in New Mexico, the state received this honor in 2000 when a 737-700 was painted yellow with a red Zia sun symbol. This aircraft, N781WN, is named *New Mexico One*. On the far right is the new control tower erected in 1994.

Volunteers for many carriers maintain a nostalgic aircraft of the past such as these Douglas DC-3s. Above is an American DC-3 named *Flagship Detroit*. This aircraft came through ABQ in 2007, while the Delta DC-3 below came through in 2002. Both aircraft provided rides to fortunate airline employees and other dignitaries. Featured with the American DC-3 are Victoria Williams and her brother, aviator John Mitros.

Eclipse Aviation was established in Albuquerque in 1998 to build the Eclipse-500 Very Light Jet shown here. The jet was certified by the Federal Aviation Administration in 2006.

A new off-site rental car facility opened in 2001, which moved all rental car operations out of the main terminal. Passengers are transported to and from the terminal by bus. Note the traditional beamed ceilings, consistent with the Albuquerque airport terminals of the past and present.

ABQ sits at an elevation of 5,352 feet above sea level (more than a mile) and is often used for high altitude testing and training, which was the case for this Air France Boeing 777-300 that visited in 2004.

ABQ sees many diverted aircraft of all types for reasons such as ill passengers, mechanical problems in flight, or severe weather at the intended destination. When nearby major hubs such as Denver and Phoenix see bad weather, many aircraft will divert to ABQ. Mexicana was a frequent visitor to the Sunport, as the airline had routes from Mexico to Denver that would fly over Albuquerque. Mexicana, a legacy carrier for Mexico since 1921, had applied to serve ABQ in 1973 but was not approved. Unfortunately, the carrier went out of business in 2010. The aircraft pictured here is an Airbus A320, seen at the Sunport in 2007.

This United Charter Boeing 747-400, parked at the Cutter Aviation ramp, came through ABQ in 2010 transporting a large military movement to Afghanistan.

This is a look at the terminal on a summer evening in 2008, when the sun lights up the north-facing front of the building most nicely.

This is a view of a busy ramp on a summer day in 2009. At that time, 11 commercial airlines were serving ABQ with a total of 117 departing flights per day.

Eight

MERGERS AND NEW TENANTS
2010s

The six major legacy airlines still operating in the United States had each merged with one another between 2010 and 2015. These mergers created excess ticket counter and gate space; however, Albuquerque city officials have been successful in recruiting four new airlines to the Sunport, the first of which was jetBlue in 2013, followed by Alaska Airlines a year later. Allegiant Air, known for its no-frills, ultra-low fare concept, began service in 2016, and Volaris Airlines of Mexico brought international service back to the Sunport in 2018. In 2017, Horizon Air, operating on behalf of Alaska Airlines as Alaska Horizon, added new flights to five cities on the west coast. All of the new carriers were given incentives such as landing-fee waivers for the first two years to provide new service to ABQ.

By 2015, passenger traffic had dropped to 4.75 million arriving and departing passengers after it had peaked in 2007 at 6.7 million. Southwest Airlines had been operating under a rule called the Wright Amendment in which all flights from its home base at Dallas Love Field were only allowed to travel to cities in states that border Texas, which includes New Mexico. That meant that many Southwest passengers from Dallas traveled to Albuquerque and then changed planes to continue anywhere farther west. The Wright Amendment was lifted in 2014, which allowed Southwest to begin nonstop flights from Dallas to points farther west, accounting for a steep decline in passengers at ABQ. Furthermore, a general trend in the public now is to drive shorter segments instead of fly, which caused Southwest to discontinue flights to cities such as Amarillo, El Paso, and Tucson. Overall, the airline reduced flights and nonstop destinations at ABQ by more than 50 percent. However, fuel prices declined during the middle of the decade, allowing airlines to reduce fares, and now traffic is on an upswing, rising to nearly 5.5 million in 2018. At the end of 2018, the total number of departing flights each day by all airlines at ABQ was 94, with nonstop service to 26 cities.

The Sunport celebrated its 75th anniversary in 2014, and the current terminal building saw its 50th year of operation in 2015. Since the last major expansion and renovation 30 years ago, the terminal is receiving a facelift that began in 2017. Once finished, it will undoubtedly be one of the most beautiful and modern airport facilities anywhere.

After 45 years, in what has to be the longest-running paint scheme of any airline, American changed its image in 2013 as it began a merger with US Airways. The carrier is also replacing its MD-80 fleet, which has served ABQ since 1985, with new Boeing 737-800s, shown here in both the old and new paint scheme. The merger with US Airways was completed in late 2015 and American now occasionally operates former US Airways aircraft through ABQ, including the Airbus A319, A320, and A321.

Mesa Airlines had been operating its fleet of CRJ-900s from Albuquerque to Phoenix as America West Express, then US Airways Express, and now as American Eagle (pictured here) with the American/US Airways merger. Other regional carriers that operate as American Eagle at ABQ include Compass, Envoy, Republic, and SkyWest. This photograph (and several more to come) was taken from an aircraft viewing area near the air-cargo facility with the Manzano Mountains in the background.

United merged with Continental in 2012 and adopted Continental's image; however, this 737-800 wears a special livery commemorating United's membership in Star Alliance, a consortium of airlines worldwide that work together to provide global service. American and Delta also belong to similar consortiums named OneWorld and SkyTeam, respectively.

United Express, operated by Republic Airlines, used this Bombardier DHC-8-402 Q400 turboprop aircraft on flights to Denver from 2012 through 2016. Along with Republic, other airlines operating as United Express at ABQ include ExpressJet, GoJet, Mesa, SkyWest, and TransStates using several types of regional jets.

Delta merged Northwest Airlines into its system in 2010, adding flights from Albuquerque to Minneapolis. Delta has been operating 757s at ABQ since 1991 but began replacing them with newer 737-900s in 2016. Seen here is a 757 in the latest "Onward and Upward" livery. The carrier occasionally operates other types of aircraft including the Airbus A319, A320, Boeing 717, and the McDonnell Douglas MD-90.

Delta Connection carrier Compass Airlines reinstated service to Los Angeles for Delta in 2017. Compass, which began as a Northwest Airlink carrier, also supplements SkyWest Airlines on the Albuquerque–Salt Lake City route with its Embraer-175s, shown here. The 76-seat Embraer-175 has become a very popular aircraft among the regional airlines operating for Delta Connection as well as for Alaska, American Eagle, and United Express.

Many airlines paint at least one of their aircraft in a retro paint scheme and also one in the colors of a past carrier that the current carrier has merged with. Seen here are an American 737-800 in the 1980s colors of TWA (above) and a United 737-900 in the "Blue Skyway" colors of Continental Airlines worn in the 1950s. As TWA and Continental were the two primary airlines serving Albuquerque for nearly 50 years, it is quite the honor to see these two particular aircraft land at the Sunport today.

Southwest introduced its largest aircraft in 2017; the new, next-generation 175-seat 737-8 Max pictured here in the latest "Heart" livery. Southwest does not have a feeder operation with regional jets like most other major airlines.

After TWA had ended nonstop flights to New York's JFK airport 32 years prior, service was reinstated by jetBlue in 2013. The once-daily flight normally arrives at ABQ around 11:00 p.m. and returns to JFK at midnight; however, on the day of this photograph, New York received heavy snowfall, causing the return flight to cancel. This Airbus A320 spent the next day in sunny Albuquerque.

Alaska Airlines began serving ABQ in 2014 with a single daily flight to Seattle using different versions of the Boeing 737. Within the first year, the carrier had settled on the largest model, the 737-900ER, shown here in a new livery that began in 2016. Albuquerque is also well known for its hot air ballooning, and occasionally, balloons will drift near the airport. Not to worry, balloon pilots are in radio communication with air traffic control.

In 2017, Alaska added new flights to five west coast cities by way of its own feeder carrier, Horizon Air, using Embraer-175 regional jets as seen here. The operation is referred to as Alaska Horizon. Alaska also has an agreement with SkyWest using Embraer-175s, which is known as Alaska SkyWest.

Allegiant Air has been operating charter flights through ABQ since 1998 and began scheduled service to Austin and Las Vegas in 2016. Flights to Los Angeles were added a short time later but ended in 2017. Allegiant only operates its flights two or three days per week and began using MD-80 aircraft, shown here, but has since switched over to Airbus A319s and A320s.

Frontier Airlines discontinued its Albuquerque service in early 2014 but returned in 2017, again with flights to Denver. Service was soon added to Austin, San Antonio, and Orlando with an ultra-low fare concept and flights that only run two or three days per week, much like Allegiant. Shown here is the new next-generation type of Airbus, the A320neo. Notice the new paint scheme, reminiscent of the old Frontier, with a stylized "F" and an arrow through the fuselage. Featured on the tail is Skye the blue jay.

On November 17, 2018, Volaris Airlines of Mexico reinstated international service to ABQ with two flights per week nonstop to Guadalajara, a sister city to Albuquerque. Pictured here is the carrier's Airbus A320 departing ABQ on its inaugural flight. Volaris also gives names to its aircraft, this one being *Los Capistrán*.

In celebration of the new service by Volaris, an excellent presentation was given in the terminal by a mariachi band and Mexican dancers performing the *jarabe tapatío*, the Mexican hat dance.

Sun Country is frequently seen at ABQ operating 737-800s on charters for sports teams as well as public charter flights to Laughlin, Nevada. Other charter air carriers regularly seen at the Sunport include Swift Air, Miami Air, Elite Airways, and Key Lime Air.

Some of the contract airlines have code-share agreements with multiple airlines, such as SkyWest, which operates as American Eagle, Delta Connection, United Express, and Alaska SkyWest, all of which serve ABQ. Most of SkyWest's aircraft are dedicated to and painted in the livery of specific airlines; however, a few aircraft, including this CRJ-700, carry SkyWest's own branding so that they may be used wherever needed.

Commuter airline Boutique Air began serving Albuquerque in 2015 with flights to Carlsbad and Silver City using the Pilatus PC-12 aircraft (left). Both routes are subsidized by the government. Boutique also briefly served Los Alamos and Alamosa in 2016 and 2017. Advanced Air was later awarded the route to Silver City and began service in early 2019 using the Beech Super King Air 350 aircraft (right).

Private charter companies that operate mostly small luxurious jets are seen daily at the general aviation facilities at ABQ. In the background on the left is a Cessna 560XL Citation XLS operated by NetJets, front and center is a Hawker Beechjet 400A flown by Flight Options, and on the right is a Cessna 750 Citation X operated by XOJet. Cutter Aviation, which services many of these aircraft, continues to thrive, now being run by the third generation of the Cutter family.

Air ambulances are constantly operating at ABQ. This Native Air Pilatus PC-12 operated by Air Methods is on duty 24 hours a day, seven days a week throughout New Mexico and neighboring states. This photograph was taken at the airport in Ruidoso, New Mexico. Many thanks are given to the captain for a tour of his aircraft and for allowing this photograph.

This Augusta Westland AW119-MKII helicopter operates as a lifeguard for the University of New Mexico Hospital in Albuquerque. Seen here at the Sunport, it also regularly lands on the hospital's rooftop.

UPS now has a much larger operation at ABQ generally running five flights per day using Airbus A300, Boeing 757, and this Boeing 767-300 aircraft taking off on runway 03. Along with flights to Louisville, the carrier now has smaller hubs at Dallas/Fort Worth, Phoenix, and Ontario, California.

FedEx operates morning and evening flights from Albuquerque to its main hub in Memphis. Along with this McDonnell Douglas DC-10 (which was first introduced in 1971), FedEx also operates Boeing 767-300, Airbus A300, and McDonnell Douglas MD-11 wide-body aircraft through ABQ.

FedEx operates its own feeder network with flights from Gallup, Farmington, and Durango. These FedEx feeders are operated by Empire Airlines using Cessna 208 Caravan aircraft.

UPS now contracts with Ameriflight and South Aero to provide feeder flights from 12 cities around New Mexico. Ameriflight operates Beech 99 and Piper Navajo aircraft while South Aero uses several versions of single and twin-engine Cessna aircraft. Shown here is an Ameriflight Beech 99. Ameriflight also operates on behalf of DHL with a flight to Phoenix.

Here is a look at the airfreight ramp on a typical early evening with several wide-body freighters. The Sandia Mountains make for a scenic backdrop.

Also based on the airfreight ramp are these DC-10 tankers, which are frequently used to battle forest fires by dropping retardant from the pods attached below. The company, 10 Tanker Air Carrier, moved its operation from California to Albuquerque in 2013.

Cavalcade of Wings, a nonprofit group founded by the late Harry Davidson to preserve the aviation history of New Mexico, has constructed and maintains an ever-growing model aircraft display inside the main terminal. Davidson was unquestionably the most knowledgeable aviation historian in the state and acquired most of the hundreds of display models, each representing an aircraft that has served or visited ABQ. Pictured here are only two of the seventeen cases on display.

Seen here ready to spin the prop (not really) is Harry Davidson in front of a Ford F-5AT tri-motor in the markings of TAT, one of the two founding carriers to provide commercial air service to Albuquerque in 1929. This photograph was taken in 2017 when the restored aircraft visited Albuquerque's Double Eagle Airport (managed by the Albuquerque International Sunport), providing nostalgic flights. Sadly, Davidson passed away while this book was in progress in 2018.

Visit us at
arcadiapublishing.com